SILVER

Silver:
An Aberdeen Anthology

ALAN SPENCE
&
HAZEL HUTCHISON

First published in 2009 by Polygon,
an imprint of Birlinn Ltd

West Newington House
10 Newington Road
Edinburgh
EH9 1QS

9 8 7 6 5 4 3 2 1

www.birlinn.co.uk

The publishers acknowledge support from

ISBN 978 1 84697 135 8

British Library Cataloguing-in-Publication Data
A catalogue record for this book is available on request
from the British Library.

Typeset in Dante by
Koinonia, Manchester
Printed and bound by
Bell & Bain Ltd, Glasgow

Contents

Old Aberdeen

Folk

A City to Learn Love In

Grey Granite

Black Gold

Scarlet Goon

Outwith

All Seasons

Introduction

It began with a poem and an anthology. The anthology was Ali Smith's wonderful compilation *The Reader*. The poem, included in that book, was Jackie Kay's 'Old Aberdeen', which was new to me and got me thinking about Aberdeen poems I'd read over the years, wondering about others I'd missed. There was the generation I grew up reading – George Bruce and Iain Crichton Smith wrote extensively about the city; there was Alexander Scott's epic 'Heart of Stone', and at the other extreme, Edwin Morgan's Chinese moment, the haiku-like 'Aberdeen Train'. Among contemporaries there was the redoubtable and prolific Sheena Blackhall, and from another hugely talented generation, Robin Robertson and Robert Crawford have worked their magic. There was more, from Roderick Watson, Ken Morrice and George Gunn. Jessie Kesson, Helen Cruickshank and Marion Angus wrote in the spik o' the place. Didn't Seamus Heaney have that line about an Aberdeen of the mind? Wasn't MacDiarmid scathing about the place in *A Drunk Man*? Byron wrote about Brig o' Balgownie in *Don Juan*, and further back again there must be something in Dunbar, in Barbour. A book began to take shape in my imagination, a collection of poems about Aberdeen, spanning the centuries. Now that would be an anthology!

My own relationship with Aberdeen goes back more than a decade. During that time I've taught creative writing at the University and dreamed up and directed the annual Word Festival. Before that I'd only ever passed through (the right idea, some friends might argue) and I had the typical Central-Belter's idea that the city was remote and dour, both in terms of geography and character. It was off the map, Ultima Thule. Here be dragons. My journey up from Edinburgh for the job interview – in December – did nothing to disabuse me, and my first bleak winter almost undid me. But like many folk I've come to love the place, its thrawnness, its harsh austere beauty, the quality of its light, its grey granite or glitter of mica, depending on the season or the time of day. (And that train journey, along the North Sea coast, is thrilling.) Aberdeen is like nowhere else, uncompromisingly and resolutely itself. When Heaney uses that expression, Aberdeen of the mind, in his poem 'Granite Chip', we know what he means. It's intriguing to see how many of the poems in this collection are titled, simply, 'Aberdeen'. The poets obviously felt that single word title was enough, indicating what George Bruce called 'this sufficient city'. These Aberdeen poems would make a fascinating collection in themselves.

There's a famous passage in Alasdair Gray's *Lanark*, where the main character, Thaw, is looking out over Glasgow, commenting on the fact that it's a beautiful city but isn't generally thought of as such because it hasn't been realised imaginatively. Duncan MacLean has a pastiche of this which has Thaw declaiming, 'Aberdeen's a beautiful city ...' and being led away in a straitjacket! Aberdonians themselves can be brutally self-mocking. I have a memory of sitting in the home stand at Pittodrie, listening to the Aberdeen support launch into a particularly virulent chant directed not against their Central Belt opposition but against themselves in a kind of pre-emptive first strike. There's plenty of harsh, male bleakness in these pages, but there's also a rare lyricism, a celebration of the city in all its moods, its shifting seasons, a sense of it, as it's described in a poem by Rachel Annand Taylor, as a city to learn love in. There's light and dark; the city is silver and grey.

At a fairly early stage in the proceedings, it became clear this anthology was going to be a joint project. I enlisted the help of a colleague, Hazel Hutchison, herself a gifted poet and a tireless researcher, whose special interest is the nineteenth century. Her first forays into the University's Library and Special Collections unearthed some rare gems – a manuscript poem by Thomas Hardy, which he had written for the University magazine, Dunbar's first-hand account of a visit to the city by Mary Queen of Scots ('Be blyth and blissfull burgh of Aberdein'). A particular favourite is a brief account by twelfth-century Icelandic poet/priest Einar Skulason, of the sacking of Aberdeen in 1153. Hazel's pitch-perfect translation ends simply, 'and Apardion fell'. This has echoes down the centuries in Edwin Morgan's wicked sonnet, 'Computer Error: Neutron Strike', which envisages the destruction of the city (by mistake!) in a nuclear blast. And it's this kind of juxtaposition, this counter-pointing, that makes an anthologist's job so enjoyable. Our decision to arrange the material not chronologically but thematically allows these connections to be made across time and between disparate writers. The city's folk/ballad tradition was also new to me, and we include two glorious examples in 'The Bonnie Lass o' Bon Accord' and 'The Bonnie Ship The *Diamond*' – you can just about smell the tang of the North Sea in that one!

When Hazel and I availed ourselves of the resources of the Scottish Poetry Library in Edinburgh – their database, their packed shelves inviting an old-fashioned rummage – we were stunned at the range and quality of the material available. There were names I knew and had come across in other contexts – Robin Munro, Gerald Mangan, Anne Stevenson – but there were other poets whose work was entirely new to me, who had appeared in magazines and anthologies and individual collections, long out of print. (A fair number of these collections were published by Aberdeen University Press. This is an imprint long overdue for revival, and perhaps this present volume, a collaboration with the Word Festival, can lead the way towards such an undertaking.) Interestingly, quite a few of these 'lost poets' were women. I was reminded at points of the work done by Tom Leonard in his *Radical Renfrew* anthology, in which he brought to light work from a fairly small community which had been forgotten, ignored or suppressed over the years

Hazel has been touched by the response of descendants of some of these poets, contacted to give permission, all delighted that the work will again appear in print. In fact everyone we contacted was happy to have their work included, and I was particularly moved to receive a note from Mick Imlah's partner just a few weeks after Mick had died, indicating that Mick had indeed read our request for permission to use his poem and that he'd been 'pleased and charmed' to be asked, and happy for us to go ahead.

For all the constancy and solidity of its granite heart, Aberdeen is a city endlessly changing. The boom years of the Black Gold – the wealth generated by North Sea oil – have come and gone. Those years are reflected in these pages – perhaps most powerfully in George Gunn's 'Piper' – but so too is all that went before, right back to that twelfth-century Icelandic monk. (I love George Mackay Brown's re-imagining of Foresterhill Hospital – where he was a patient in the 1980s – as a mediaeval monastery, a place of healing for body and soul.) What excites me about this anthology is that sense it gives of Aberdeen's history, and its cultural life, over many centuries. The University – now in its sixth century – has been central to that life, and we make no apologies for the section entitled 'Scarlet Goon', taking its title from a poem by Jessie Kesson. I'm also glad to report that University poets are flourishing, and we include (on merit) work by some of our colleagues on campus – Peter Davidson, Christine Laennec, Wayne Price, Thomas Rist and Tim Tricker. Add to these contributions by some of the poets who have graced local writers' groups over the years, from the Lemon Tree and Books & Beans – Gerard Rochford, Eddie Gibbons, Sue Vickerman – and we have a reminder that really good work is still being written in the city and inspired by it.

A. S.

When I moved to Aberdeen, I knew very little about it. I was twenty-one and knew very little about anything, although that wasn't how I saw it at the time. I came in September at the start of a long, misty autumn, and I was ready to start something new. I fell in love with the place almost at once: with the haar that blurred the lean lines of the buildings and muffled the sounds of the city like snow; with the clear, sharp air and the pale northern light; with the acres of civic roses; with the rich, open farmland of Aberdeenshire scraped bare for harvest; with the short November afternoons where the sun hung low in the sky for hours; with the thick town accent and its strange, new vocabulary; with rowies, and cassies, and louns, and fine pieces. Even the sound of the gulls and the midnight oyster-catchers was magical and distinctive. But, as with every romance, there was also a lot that I didn't know at the start, and a lot to get used to. This city has a raw side, a remote side, a harsh and relentless side – perhaps everywhere does. But in Aberdeen the lovable and the bleak are so closely intertwined that many people never manage to tell them apart. If you live here, then you probably know what I mean. If you don't then it isn't easy to explain.

Cities like people are hard to pin down. No sooner have you said something conclusive about them than they come up with something unexpected just to prove you wrong. Rather than trying to reason it out, perhaps what you need is a metaphor, and for this city the metaphor that you need is the very stuff of which the place is made – granite. Bleak, grey, uncompromising, solid, durable, reliable and weirdly beautiful when seen up close in the right kind of light – it is hard to separate the city from its primary building material. And why would you want to? This is the Granite City, after all. In fact many of the things that you can say about Aberdeen start with this basic element. There is a lot of granite here. The granite is very grey. It is not exactly a warm place – not at any rate in the meteorological sense. Lewis Grassic Gibbon, one of the region's most famous literary sons, wrote that living in Aberdeen was 'comparable to passing one's existence in a refrigerator'. And, yes, the nights are very long in the winter. But then again, the days are just as long in the summer, and the granite really does sparkle silver in sunlight, and on a clear morning with a light breeze whipping in off the North Sea, there are few places in the world where you can feel half so alive.

For a long time I worried that my double-sided feelings about Aberdeen were a sign of failing to adjust to my new environment – but quite the opposite. The longer I live here, the more I realise that most people feel like this about the place, even those who have never lived anywhere else. It is a city of contrasts. On a Friday night in Union Street, Aberdeen seems like a rough, hard-drinking, night-clubbing town, but then you find yourself, ice-cream in hand, at Duthie Park on a summer Sunday afternoon, watching grannies pushing prams and fellows in whites playing cricket on the grass. Coming home on the train from the south, as the carriage gradually empties out at station after station, you feel like you live at the end of the world, but then you listen to the many different languages spoken on the High Street, or you look at the names of the home ports on the boats in the harbour, and you realise how tightly linked this city is to a vast global network of commerce and culture.

This anthology shows how many others have been through a similar set of conflicting emotions about Aberdeen. Many poems, such as those by Ian Crichton Smith, Sue Vickerman and William Watson, deal with first impressions of the city, with the baffling charm which counteracts its stony grandeur. And those who stay long enough, a lifetime perhaps, continue to be bewildered by its paradoxical qualities, its elusiveness – which is odd for a place famed for its rocky solidity. Marion Angus, Alexander Scott, George Bruce, Roderick Watson, and many more, celebrate the multiple personalities of the city. And I suspect it is this sense of its infinite variety that makes Aberdeen so difficult, sooner or later, not to love. As Grassic Gibbon observed in the 1930s, even those who detest Aberdeen do so 'with the detestation of a thwarted lover'. He concludes, 'It is the one haunting and exasperatingly lovable city in Scotland – its fascination as unescapable as its shining mail.'

Aberdeen proudly presents itself as a commercial and industrial hub – which of course it is. Since the discovery of North Sea Oil in the 1960s, the city has changed dramatically. Traditional industries such as fishing, ship-building and textiles have been swept away in the wake of the changes and the money that the oil has brought. The area around Aberdeen is now one of the richest regions in Europe – although you certainly wouldn't guess this from looking at some bits of the city. But there has always been much more happening here than the drive towards prosperity. One of the hidden aspects of the city is the richness of its literary heritage. This tends to be overlooked because of Aberdeen's distance and difference from the areas to which the Scottish nation usually turns to reinforce its sense of self: the Central Belt to the south, and the Highlands and Islands to the west. Indeed, the deep and distinctive culture of the North-East is one of Scotland's best kept secrets. So well-kept is this secret, in fact, that many Aberdonians are unaware of the resources buried beneath their own feet. Most Grampian schoolchildren are given Grassic Gibbon's novel *Sunset Song* to read at some stage, and no one who attends Aberdeen Grammar School is allowed to forget that Byron did too, but fewer people know that John Barbour (c. 1320–95) was the 'father of Scottish poetry', or that Thomas Hardy travelled here in 1905 to receive an honorary doctorate from the University of Aberdeen and celebrated the city in verse. But almost more impressive than the city's many connections to the A-list of literature is the depth of creative artistry that has been quietly at work here through the centuries.

When this project began, in an attempt to balance Alan's exceptional knowledge of contemporary Scottish writing, I took myself to the library (several libraries, in fact) to see what I could find that had been forgotten. I explored the collections of the University of Aberdeen where I work, visited the Aberdeen Central Library on Rosemount Viaduct, and spent several happy afternoons in the Scottish Poetry Library on the Royal Mile in Edinburgh, eating custard creams and ranging through their catalogue. The results were extraordinary. Volume after volume of verse called out for attention, many by writers of whom I had never heard: Agnes Carnegie, W. F. McCorkindale, Rachel Annand Taylor, Ronald Campbell MacFie, Arthur Geddes. Having worried that we would have to work to find enough material for a slim volume, Alan and I suddenly found ourselves looking for ways to contain the sheer weight of poetry that presented itself. Thus, for every poem in this volume there are many more that we passed over, often for fairly arbitrary reasons. For example, we decided to draw a tight line around the city boundaries, ignoring almost everything about the countryside and the mountains beyond. Many long poems such as MacFie's 'Marischal College' or Scott's 'Heart of Stone' were ruthlessly filleted to provide bite-sized portions. And there are probably many more works about the city that we did not even find. So, readers should remember that this collection constitutes only the tip of a large poetic iceberg, and if it prompts anyone to go in search of some of the poems we *didn't* select, then the book will have served a fine purpose. But the poems that are here seem to us (and we could hardly believe how closely we agreed on what to put in and what to leave out) to be the pick of the crop, chosen to create a vivid picture of the city as it is in the early twenty-first century – modern, urban, international and yet deeply rooted in its own history and culture.

All the same, it is surely a mistake to imagine that this picture will stand still for long. I have spent twenty years trying to work out how I feel about Aberdeen and I'm not done yet. Perhaps this is because the city itself is always in flux, not set in stone after all, but alive and evolving. More discoveries and changes lie in wait, no doubt, and more poems to catch these as they unfold. If nothing else, working on this anthology has reminded me that this city always has something unexpected up its silver sleeve.

H. H.

Boast

Anon

Aberdeen an twal mile round.
Fife and aa the lands about it,
Taen fae Scotland's runklet map,
Little's left, and wha's tae doubt it?

Silver City

Aberdeen

Iain Crichton Smith

Mica glittered from the white stone.
Town of the pure crystal,
I learnt Latin in your sparkling cage,
I loved your brilliant streets.

Places that have been good to us we love.
The rest we are resigned to.
The fishermen hung shining in their yellow
among university bells.

Green lawns and clinging ivy. Medieval
your comfortable lectures, your calm grammar.
The plate glass windows showed their necklaces
like writhing North Sea fish.

Nothing will die, even the lies we learn!
Union Street was an arrow
debouching on the crooked lanes, where women
sweated like leaking walls.

Aberdeen

Thomas Hardy

'And wisdom and knowledge shall be the stability of thy times.'
Isaiah 33, v.6.

I looked; and thought, 'She is too gray and cold
To wake the warm enthusiasms of old!'
Till a voice passed: 'Behind that granite mien
Lurks the imposing beauty of a Queen.'
I looked anew; and saw the radiant form
Of Her who stays in stress, who guides in storm;
On the grave influence of whose eyes sublime
Men count for the stability of the time.

The Don

Harry Smart

I grew up here, among the stones;
among the stones and the willow trees
where I could watch the water rise
in the river and fall. It was sweet
water here, too far from the river's mouth
for the salt wedge to reach, the tide's
thin tongue on the top of the river.

Except now and again, on a big tide
when the stream bulked like a black back,
we'd catch a salty breath that said sun
and moon were pulling together. Stretching
the invisible membrane, interface
where salt and sweet met skin to skin,
they lay against each other, reaching

a mile or more in from the sea; two
cold waters flowing in two directions,
different, separate, each unbroken,
and the mass of the river piling.

North East Toun

Sheena Blackhall

Stars skinkle ower a parkin lot
Hubcaps an bonnets shine wi frost
Like mowdies, weariet shoppers skail
Oot frae the mall, bood doon bi cost
O stappin stammachs, heatin hames.
Twa bats gae flichterin fae the trees
Raggety cloots o hungered wames.

Ice surfs the waves. Black spires luik doon
Icicle kirks in this cauld toon
An hoasts hack deeper in the briest
O fowk fa thole the cauld the least
Slipt somehou frae the shelterin goun
O him fa wore the thorny croun.

Aberdeen

Robert Crawford

Port of the re-used Christmas card,
Capital of Doric oil,

Your reputation sluices beyond you,
Shetland's gateway to the south,

Global dorp, helipad of the Shore Porters,
Your undeflectably local paper's

Cobbled headline when the *Titanic* sank,
'Aberdeen Man Drowned.'

Loud on the left side of Scotland's breast,
You are my country's hardened heart,

Macho, Calgachan, missing a beat
Down Union Street, or out on the rigs,

But leaping up, handbagged by laughter
At the Fun Beach's northern lights.

I love your hard core, Marischal College,
Town Hall and tenements, stunner after stunner

Howked out of the Rubislaw Quarry's
Undiamondiferous granite.

The Silver City

Marion Angus

Yonder she sits beside the tranquil Dee,
Kindly yet cold, respectable and wise,
Sharp-tongued though civil, with wide-open eyes,
Dreaming of hills, yet urgent for the sea;
And still and on, she has her vanity,
Wears her grey mantle with a certain grace,
While sometimes there are roses on her face
To sweeten too austere simplicity.

She never taught her children fairy lore,
Yet they must go a-seeking crocks of gold
Afar throughout the earth;
And when their treasure in her lap they pour,
Her hands upon her knee do primly fold;
She smiles complacent that she gave them birth.

City Shape

Robin Munro

The City is inside me.
The City transport system
moves my brain, till the last
scheduled plane has threatened Mastrick
and the stars set sail.

Then late, late, under an old moon,
go, as a park turns graveyard,
to the Summer Hill
with sodium daisies.

City soil is sore in need of light.
From the Lang Stracht to the North Field
see the shape groan upwards
like a buried thing.

My theme:
the whole suppression of the singing way.
My statement:
one day Don and Dee will rise,
the roses that were wild thorn once
will cease to be contained in ring road roundabouts,
Beach Boulevards will side with sea, and links
and parks, and such as we.

Aberdeen

Kevin MacNeil

Union St. The Lemon Tree.
Diamond St. How the sun
sparks off this granite city –
dharmadhatu, bright as you,
your smile, the light in your ever
changing, ever warm, ripening
eyes, like wild fruits, like a million
mica stars coming alive; your
near heat and dazzle shows me
I'm closer to Lewis, closer to source,
a zendo of mirrors and torches
flashing directly, limitless and spontaneous.

Aiberdeen Street

Alastair Mackie

I

Ye were hyne awa fae Nuremberg o the flags,
the death-crap o the purges; Il Duce's
black-sarked legions heistin eagles …
Woolie's guns and gairden canes airmed oor wars
focht on your cassies, oor granite battle-field.
Paper planes whitent the gloamin-faa,
earth-bund swallas the scaffies sweepit up.
And quines were bobbin corks aneth the tow brigs
o their skippin ropes. Cairt horses snochert
and the shod wheels girned and dirded.
Here in this play-grun atween the tenements
– sea gulls on the lums – I breathed in Scots.
Years later I howkit up the street's kist
o memories and found amon the mools, deid words,
the affcasts o history, teuch as granite setts,
the foonds o my world.

II

The navel-tow o the street,
I snippit ye lang syne for war, for college,
for a dominie's day darg … Your skirling lung
is quaiter nou, cloggit up wi metal.
(I mauna cuddle in the wyme o yesterdays.)
The granite tenements stand yet
faur streenger fowk bide nou. Windas like glowerers
gaup still on oor auld hoose,
the granite centenarian o the street.
The place is like a kirk-yaird.
Fae the dowier distances o middle age
aathing's smaaer than it used to be.

My father crines at the het cheek o the ingle,
and oot the winda, a tooer block
rents the air.
      Ower the chippit cassies
the tackety beets o deid louns thinly jow.

III

Nae McD's 'lang coffin o a street',
mair a village fit-path lined wi setts.
Streets at tap and boddom merked oor frontiers.
We spoke o girds, scuds, quines, bleedy doctors …
I'm richt glad the auld words still come back
like migrant swallas, black shears o the gloamin.
Marx we hadna heard o, only the Marx brithers.
This was oor grunwork, the hard pan o oor lives.
A sma bit street that hirpled doun a brae.
Whitever roads I took since then I
began wi workin fowk in granite tenements.
Aa the lave was superstructure.

To Aberdeen

William Watson

At the great dance and upleap of the year
      I came. For me, the northwind's cold accost
      Was all day long in thy warm welcome lost.
How should I fail henceforth to hold thee dear?
Hoary thy countenance and thy mien severe,
      And built of the bones of Mother Earth thou wast.
      But on thy heart hath fall'n no touch of frost,
O city of the pallid brow austere.
Grey, wintry-featured, sea-throned Aberdeen!
      The stranger thou hast honoured shall not cease,
      In whatsoever ways he rest or roam,
To wish thee noble fortune, fame serene:
      Thee and thy towers of learning and of peace,
      That brood benignant on the northern foam.

King Street

Thomas Rist

After a while,
The stink of fish
Begins to pale.

The grey looks silver
In sky, granite
And still haar,

And the dirty gulls
Beneath midnight lights
Seem whitened souls.

Exchange your new
TV for a black-and-white.
You will make do.

Walk from Fittie
To Bridge of Don.
You'll warm to the city.

Dark Grey Sea

Envoi

George Bruce

Go, drama of wind, water and stone,
Drama of men long under granite lid.
Go to those with abundant energy
Whose eyes lift to the hard North light.
Go to those shaken by the petulant sea.

Aberdeen

Gerald Mangan

A grey slick of gulls on the swell.
The smell of fish and whisky
hanging like spindrift,
and a spark of frost in the stone,

where the stone rebuffs the sea:
proof against all the fustian
the sea throws in its face.
It won't stand for fancy stuff,

and won't give an inch
to the wind, or the chisel.
It knows its mind so well,
it hardly needs to speak it:

standing sound as ever,
in a dream of ice and brimstone.
It's the sea, without the oil,
that ground its edge like this.

Port of Aberdeen

W. F. McCorkindale

There is little reticence about this harbour
with gaping hold and open hatch revealing all
as long-necked iron cranes
fastidiously peck among the cargoes
        fetch gratifying morsels
for gourmandising trucks and greedy trailers.

The buzz-saw in a builder's yard
like vespa vulgaris caught and held
        shot down
in the beam of an aerosol spray
adds its unmistakable voice
        to the pandemonic industry
of mid-morning bustle and bash among men
who are the masters, after all, to some extent.

Yet they who made the whole thing possible
        including the débris
are strangely minor to the presence of the ships,
        are hopelessly upstaged –
as in the railway days of steam
few would ask the engine driver's name –
and *Ferryhill* of Aberdeen gives birth to coal
        in a gargantuan Caesarean
(howling like Fenriswulf at the gates
        of Hel his sister)
and never a man is moving where she lies
among a ruination of baskets boards and boxes
a flotsam refuse dump around Atlantic Wharf.

A deep-sea trawler brays departure,
with softly popping noises slips away
and 528 on quarter throttle pulses,
      simulating eagerness to reach
some teeming El Dorado of the fishing grounds
while yellow loaders nibble bite and gorge
at their appointed meals of pine and teak
spruce and cedar regimentally disposed
      along the cobbled shore.

Trojan, of tremendous self-importance,
bustles to an outer anchorage
prepared to put all new arrivals
      firmly in their place,
and the tourist-weary Shetland steamer
      snoozes for a time
regaining her composure now that winter
sickens off the restless voyagers to summer isles.

Nearby *Craighall* with her buckled plates
      and rusty mast askew
battered by some nameless Titan of the depths
      some blundering assailant
deep in a jungle of tall seas,
rises and falls with no resistance
      or resentment
forlorn by Clement's Bridge
in sluggish swirls of oil, french letters,
      shattered spars and crumpled cans,
abandoned for a while by men
who were the masters after all, to some extent.

Spectrum painted by the moving sun
in slicks of oil by Blaikie's Quay
trails ribbons of its chocolate-boxy hues

to shed and sawdust, fish and fuel,
and rubber-aproned, rubber-booted
      fishmen and women
knee-deep in wagonloads of shattered
      ice and salt:
to *Andrea Ursula* of Bremen,
Etly Dainielsen, Dedowsk, Discovery,
      Kisolaru Maru,
that confer on loungers and industrious alike
an accolade of that freemasonry that's shared
      by all who fare upon the seas –
men who are the masters, after all,
of whether they go or stay, to some extent.

Fishmarket

W. F. McCorkindale

In the banshee nights of northern gales
Port-red and starboard green
Pitch in the cold of winter;
Under moonlight, under deck-light
Cod and haddock, plaice and sole,
Are bronze and silver, copper and gold
For the maw of a granite market.

Where the raucous gulls will scream
                and swoop and snatch
As strident fishmen call the tune
Of price and weight and bid
That soars among the leafless spars
And branches of black masts against the sun
And smokestack stumps and chimneys
Above the tackle rattle
The creak of line and sigh of rope.

But sometimes in a clammy stillness,
Sea calm, gulls silent, traders gone,
Through the shimmer of evening
Over the oil-dark water comes
A melody so razor-thin it is not heard
But felt as a chill along the spine
Of loneliness abroad an empty ocean

And indifferent death
Beneath an Arctic sky.

The Herring Are Come

John Sinclair

Mountainous silver monotony
of fish, harboured,
wag and flounder
out of boxes,
like trinkets
dangling.
They are ready now
for monger's marble
and deft knife tracing
round the bones.
Seagulls hover,
hanging angelic predators,
picking fish heads,
eyes still swimming.
4/6 is market price
of fish flesh,
dead, but freshly.
White coat surgeon salesmen
mentally dissect their wares;
the herring are come.

Buntàt' is Sgadan

Meg Bateman

Chaidh an dàn seo a chur ri chèile air prògram Choinnich, air cuspair
a thug Aonghas Dubh seachad, Là na Bàrdachd 2004.

Tha cuimhne agam air praisean mòra dhiubh
am measg nan oileanach an Obar Dheadhain –
sùgh glas, buntàt' glas, èisg ghlas,
's iad a' coimhead a-mach à àite
an leòm fhuar a' Great Northern Hotel,
is na h-oileanaich gan slugadh,
gu h-obann balbh, a' smaoineachadh air an dachaigh...
ach cha do bhlais mise orra.

'S tha cuimhne agam air bodach sa chidsin
an Griomasaigh, is barail fa chomhair,
is e a' reubadh ceann is mionaich dhiubh le aon char,
fuil, salann is sùilean air feadh an àite,
is cha do bhlais mi orra sin na bu mhotha.

Ach nan toireadh tus', Aonghais Dhuibh,
truinnsear dhiubh an-dràsta dhomh,
dh'itheamaid còmhla iad
mar urram air na h-igheanan
a chutadh trì fichead dhiubh sa mhionaid
is gàir' air an aodann,
's air an iomadh cuimhne agads' nach eil agams' orra,
air a' bhuntàta gu dìomhair ag at san ùir,
air bolg an èisg a' fàs cruinn sa mhuir
is air ar càirdeas fhèin
a' fàs nas reamhra leis an aois.

Tatties and Herring

Meg Bateman

This poem was composed on Coinneach Mòr's programme on a subject given out by 'Black Angus', National Poetry Day 2004.

I remember the students in Aberdeen
with great pots of them –
grey broth, grey tatties, grey fish,
looking out of place in the cold
splendour of the Great Northern Hotel,
and they, suddenly silent,
wolfing them down, thinking of home ...
but I didn't touch them.

And I remember the old man in the kitchen
in Grimsay, a barrel set before him,
cutting off heads and guts with one swift move,
blood, salt and eyes flying everywhere,
and I didn't touch those either.

But if you, Black Angus,
brought me a plate of them just now,
we'd eat them together,
as a homage to the girls
who'd gut sixty a minute
with a smile on their faces,
to your memories of them that are not mine,
to potatoes swelling in the dark earth,
to fishes' bellies getting round in the sea,
and to our own friendship
growing plumper through the years.

Aberdeen

Robin Robertson

The grey sea turns in its sleep
disturbing seagulls from the green rock.

We watched the long collapse, the black drop
and frothing of the toppled wave; looked out
on the dark that goes to Norway.

We lay all night in an open boat, that rocked
by the harbour wall – listening to the tyres creak
at the stone quay, trying to keep time –
till the night-fishers came in their arc, their lap
of light: the fat slap of waves, the water's
sway, the water mullioned with light.

The sifting rain, italic rain; the smirr
that drifted down for days; the sleet.
Your hair full of hail, as if sewn there.
In the damp sheets we left each other sea-gifts,
watermarks: long lost now in all these years
of the rip-tide's swell and trawl.

All night the feeding storm banked up
the streets and houses. In the morning
the sky was yellow, the frost ringing.

The grey sea turns in its sleep
disturbing seagulls from the green rock.

Nigg
Ken Morrice

Time alone separates the dull red
Granite of these cliffs and the red
Clay in the kirkyard yonder.
As I stand on this gray day,
With scarce a breath to sunder
The wetness of air and sea,
Let my living and my dead
Surround me. Let them say
Who carried the sea upon his back,
What fish sucked the marrow from whose bones,
Drifting like the untidy sea-wrack,
Whose blood seeps now to colour the clay
Of the ploughed field and the crimson cliff.

I would have written an epitaph
To please them and to honour the good,
The mortal drudgery, the valour
That lies now beneath the cold wet gravestones.
But the whistling peewit mocks my mood.
And anyway they would not have understood.

The Bonnie Ship the *Diamond*

Anon

The *Diamond* is a ship, brave boys,
    For Davis Straits she's bound,
And the quay it is all garnished
    With pretty girls around.
Captain Gibbons gives command
    To sail the oceans high,
Where the sun it never sets, brave boys,
    Nor darkness dims the sky.

    So be cheerful, my lads,
        Let your courage never fail,
    While the bonnie ship the *Diamond*
        Goes a-fishing for the whale.

Along the quay at Aberdeen
    The girlies they do stand,
With their mantles all around them,
    And the salt tears running down.
Don't weep my pretty, fair maids,
    Though you be left behind;
For the rose will grow on Greenland's ice
    Before we change our mind.

    So be cheerful, etc.

Oh, joyful will be the days
    When the Greenland lads come home;
For they are men of honour,
    Of bravery and renown.
They wear the trousers of the white,
    The jacket of the blue;

And when they come to Aberdeen
     They'll get sweethearts enew.

     So be cheerful, etc.

Oh, jovial will be the days
     When our Greenland lads come home;
For they are men of honour,
     Belonging to the town.
They'll make the cradles for to rock,
     The blankets for to wear;
And the girlies into Aberdeen
     Sing, 'Hushie-ba, my dear.'

     So be cheerful, etc.

Here's a health unto the *Hercules*,
     Another to the *Jane*,
Here's a health unto the *Bon-Accord*,
     The *Diamond* by her lane;
Here's a health unto the *Bon-Accord*,
     The *Diamond* and her crew;
Here's a health unto each bonnie lass
     That's got a heart so true.

     So be cheerful, my lads,
          Let your courage never fail,
     While the bonnie ship the *Diamond*
          Goes a-fishing for the whale.

Setting Out

Peter Mowat

I describe the incident exactly as it happened,
Only there was no incident, not really,
Just an event. Events are what happen all the time,
Even to you they happen. It is what our life is made of,
It is what my life is made of, most of the time.

This event happened in a pub, with a sign on the door
Which said: 'No Ladies'. The sign on the door is irrelevant,
Except insofar as there were no ladies present, and
That too is irrelevant. Picture yourself in this ordinary
Public House. Picture me if it is easier. A small public house.

There is a picture on one of the walls, a painting. The painting
Is of a small fishing boat, setting out from a grey pier
To the dark grey sea beyond. Now and then a red dart flies
Past this picture on its way to the dartboard. There are
Other pictures, none of them are good; neither is the one you are
                                                    looking at.

The small man on your left, age about sixty, wearing a grey coat,
Unaware of his Aberdeen accent, is the small man who painted
The picture you were looking at, a minute ago; only now you are
Looking at him. He is unaware of you, but very aware of his
                                                    picture
On the wall. In fact he is talking about it, this very minute, in his
                                                    Aberdeen accent.

I describe the incident exactly as it happened. Most of it
You already know. You know the accent of the hero, only
There was no hero, not really. Events are what your life
Is made of, not heroes. The painting is of a small fishing boat,
Setting out for the dark grey sea.

Old Aberdeen

Apardjón, 1153

Einarr Skúlason

Frétt hef k, at fell
– folks brustu svell –
– jöfurr eyddi frið –
Apardjónar lið.

I have heard tell
– that like ice sheets swords shattered –
– the prince destroyed peace –
and Apardion fell.

Aberdeen

Agnes C. Carnegie

I think looking over the town how these remain,
Mountains and sea, that west and east have been
Its bastions since primeval brown and green,
Broken and gouged, first furnished man's domain,
How shore and mountain cave could not contain
His lot, how saints gave potency to glean
Harvests of soul and flesh these streams between –
Machar his church, Fotin his fishermen.
Here men have stood, years, centuries ago,
On light-drenched days, and drawn deep breath as I
To see these mountains with their glinting snow,
A brooding city wall to landward lie,
This changing sea in changeless boundary flow
From cliffs and curves of shore to the far sky.

from Legends of the Saints: Machor

Anon

sancte machore thane thankfully
his gyft tuk, & all the place by
socht to & fra, til he fand
a sted til hyme wes gannand,
besyd a water bank, that rane
in-to the se, & lyk was thane
as It a byschopis staf had bene.
& fra sancte machore had It sene,
til his disciplis can he say:
'lo! here myn dwelling place for ay,
for my master to me cane tel,
that I in sik a place suld dwel.'
then gert he bygyne thare be mad
til him as he mystere had.
& syne til al the lawe gert he
bygyne mak in thare degree.
& eftyr that he gert wyrk
be craftly men a costlyk kyrk,
and that men callyt yet,
'of sancte machore the seg ore set.'

The Old Bridge of Dee
Agnes C. Carnegie

This cloudy stillness over the full river
Bare trees and dull grass snow-sodden,
Before the darkening of the March evening,
Receives you, grey and lichened bridge more kindly
Than busy midday's cold clear light,
Restores the landscape of your sober beauty
That in an alien world lives out its days.

Here to your slender span the wide highways
Bring the discharge of cities, the lorry passes
In the old path of rider and vagabond,
Careless of ribbed and rounded arch, of turret,
Parapet worn, walls heraldic and hoary;
And here the clamour from a race-track echoes
Over the place where your Lady Chapel stood.

But now the brooding air gathers, untroubled,
Voices friendly and fleeting into its dream,
Chatter of gulls, an oyster-catcher's piping,
The song a thrush begins for the spring's coming,
The laugh of a girl crossing beside her lover,
Voices across your centuries vibrating
Above the river's ancient monotone.

These have been with you always, were before you,
Binding with tenuous threads the weft of ages,
Mingled now with murmurs from scenes of dream,
Footfall of horse and beggar, peasant and pilgrim,
Tapping of mason's chisel, blessing of bishop,
Clacking of kingsman's sword on Covenanter's,
Voices of queen and herdsman, player and peer.

To Aberdein

William Dunbar

Blyth Aberdeane, thow beriall of all tounis,
  The lamp of bewtie, bountie, and blythnes;
Unto the heaven [ascendit] thy renoun is
  Off vertew, wisdome, and of worthines;
  He nottit is thy name of nobilnes,
Into the cuming of oure lustie Quein,
  The wall of welth, guid cheir and mirrines:
Be blyth and blisfull, burgh of Aberdein.

And first hir mett the burges of the toun
  Richelie arrayit, as become thame to be,
Of quhom they cheset four men of renoun,
  In gounes of velvot, young, abill, and lustie,
  To beir the paill of velves cramase
Abone hir heid, as the custome hes bein;
  Gryt was the sound of the artelyie:
Be blyth and blisfull, burgh of Aberdein.

Anc fair processioun mett hir at the Port,
  In a cap of gold and silk, full pleasantlie,
Syne at hir entrie, with many fair disport,
  Ressaveit hir on streittis lustilie;
  Quhair first the Salutatioun honorabilly
Of the sweitt Virgin guidlie mycht be seine;
  The sound of menstrallis blawing to the sky:
Be blyth and blisfull, burgh of Aberdein.

And syne thow gart the orient kingis thrie
  Offer to Chryst, with benyng reverence,
Gold, sence, and mir, with all humilitie,
  Schawand him king with most magnificence;
  Syne quhow the angill, with sword of violence,

Furth of the joy of paradice putt clein
    Adame and Ev for innobedience:
Be blyth and blisfull, burcht of Aberdein.

And syne the Bruce, that evir was bold in sto[u]r,
    Thow gart as roy cum rydand under croun,
Richt awfull, strang, and large of portratour,
    As nobill, dreidfull, michtie campioun:
    The [nobill Stewarts] syne, of great renoun,
Thou gart upspring, with branches new and greine,
    Sa gloriouslie, quhill glaidid all the toun:
Be blyth and blisfull, burcht of Aberdein.

Syne come thair four and tuentie madinis ying,
    All claid in greine of mervelous bewtie,
With hair detressit, as threidis of gold did hing,
    With quhyt hattis all browderit rycht brav[elie,]
    Playand on timberallis and syngand rycht sweitlie;
That seimlie sort, in ordour weill besein,
    Did meit the Quein, hir [saluand] reverentlie:
Be blyth and blisfull, burcht of Aberdein.

The streittis war all hung with tapestrie,
    Great was the pres of peopill dwelt about,
And pleasant padgeanes playit prattelie;
    The legeis all did to thair Lady loutt,
    Quha was convoyed with ane royall routt
Of gryt barrounes and lustie ladyis schene;
    Welcum, our Quein! the commones gaif ane schout:
Be blyth and blisfull, burcht of Aberdein.

At hir cuming great was the mirth and joy,
    For at thair croce aboundantlie rane wyne;
Untill hir ludgeing the toun did hir convoy;
    Hir for to treit thai sett thair haill ingyne,

Ane riche present thai did till hir propyne,
Ane costlie coup that large thing wald contene,
　　Coverit and full of cunyeitt gold rycht fyne:
Be blyth and blisfull, burcht of Aberdein.

O potent princes, pleasant and preclair,
　　Great caus thow hes to thank this nobill toun,
That, for to do the honnour, did not spair
　　Thair geir, riches, substance, and persoun,
　　The to ressave on maist fair fasoun;
The for to pleis they socht all way and mein;
　　Thairfour, sa lang as Quein thow beiris croun,
Be thankfull to this burcht of Aberdein.

from Roull of Costorphine

Stewart Conn

He has taen Roull of Aberdene,
And gentill Roull of Corstorphin,
Twa better fallowis did no man see
Timor mortis conturbat me.
> *William Dunbar, 'Lament for the Makars'*

To his Cousin in Aberdene

I retain mellow memories of your visit
and of learning much from you, anent
metre and rhyme. And seeing as I do
poetry's prime purpose as the interplay
of nature and the affections, trust in return
you will elevate your subject-matter:
I'd hate future exchanges between us
to degenerate into flytings, even in fun.

As to health, I hope neither of us will require
the visitor whose repertoire takes in the severing
of limbs and opening of the body's cavities:
diet of sweet herbs rather, to ease our ageing.
That is to say, despite rubbing shoulders
with Physics and Barber-Surgeons, I aim
not to let them practise on me – but quietly
to pursue my chronicling of the seasons.

And in an indeterminate age (heather-clumps lit
to keep my house decontaminate) give thanks
for a loving wife's contours, sons grown
to manhood; content here at Corstophin. From
a nearby doocot, a constant whoo-whoo-ing.
As for immortality: the Makars' flowering
ensures our generation will never be forgotten,
timor mortis non *conturbat me ...*

His Cousin's Reply

Delighted to hear there is life
in the old dog yet, your wife
a sweet haven for your
desires. Have no fears
regarding my verse: the great
Dunbar I too prefer when aureate.
But high on my list, such scoundrels
as steal my capons and fat fowls.

Cursit and wareit be their werd
quhyll they be levand on this erd;
hunger, sturt, and tribulation,
and never to be without vexation …
povertie, pestilence or poplexy
I wish them, dum deif as edropsy,
the cruke, the cramp, the colica,
the dry boak, &c. &c …

My stay vivid in the mind's eye,
several new poems at half-cock
describing the Castle on its Rock.
But I grew leery at the notion
of a royal tooth extraction.
Nor could I settle in Corstorphin:
after Aberdeen I need the sea –
its smash and sigh soothing to me.

But now I am home again
what hurts is the derision
of those who cry 'Butter fingers'
at my pig's bladder blunders.
How convey what hackers
they were who routed us?
But let them venture north,
by God we'll stuff them.

from Foresterhill (1992)

George Mackay Brown

In the spring and early summer of 1990 I was a patient at Foresterhill, the Aberdeen Royal Infirmary. To pass the time, I worked on a sequence of poems, imagining a medieval monastic beginning for Foresterhill. I was trying to express some gratitude, too, to the surgeons, doctors, and nursing staff. I finished the draft of the sequence at Balfour Hospital in Orkney, before coming home.

Cutting Down Trees

In a clearing of trees
      (Cut down twenty trees)
Here let it be built, the hut
      Near a well, with a hearthstone.
  We can spare two brothers
  One with healing in his hands
  One with a psalter interleaved with herbs.
It may be, the sick man
That fled from the stones into the heart of the forest
  Will seek the fire
  And will be there still when morning sifts through the branches.

Architect

Macher, architect, built merchants' houses.
Last month, a villa at Dee-mouth for a skipper's widow,
Five crowns in purse for that work.
Soon, in farms, the fever-fire.
This mason, master of the granite hewing, squaring, last
    pure chiselling, cold star glitters,
'There must be cool place, infirmaria,
Pines that have lately known snow
Where they bide till the roses of sickness wither.'
See, this drawing on a hide: *Macher made this* inscribed.

Healer

Gift of Wholeness, blossoming, the dance
Of air, stone, rain.
I think of Eck, his blundering
With pen and scroll – such blots – in the library.
No, he could not wash a floor
But the bucket was upset.
The voice of Eck a crow at Matins and Vespers.
Weed the herb garden, Eck. Weeds only
Infested the plot.
We must send Eck back soon
To his father and the fishing boat at Catterline.

In the diversity of gifts, for Eck
Nothing, a stone on his palm.

At Foresters' Hill, our infirmary there
Eck found rare roots in the burn
We hadn't known before.
Virtue flowed from Eck's fingers
Into abscess and lesion.
The lepers cry, 'We'll have Eck for bandaging, brothers.'

So we may see, dear people
Blessings may break from stone, who knows how.

A Scroll

Sun faileth not
    Pouring our cornstalks and honey
        From the golden jar.
Moon never fails, the shifting silver of the plate
        A-jostle with fish.

Stars not fail, the fleece and cargoes
        Be ushered home under Hesper.

    *

The lantern at our gatepost will soon be out.
The candles over our beds of suffering, they will be cold
wax in time.
The refectory fire a smoke-blackened stone.
*

A holy man had written:
Prayers, charities, alms, blessings
These be the little flames
Outlasting diamond and emerald and the star-in-the-granite.

Comings and Goings
Where do you go from here, traveller?
Ruddy in the cheek again, I go seeking a harvest fee
in Echt.

Do you go on far, traveller?
To Catterline, with a cart to buy fish, now the fever has
left me.

You will leave us so soon, traveller?
Yes, I can hammer nails again in the boatyard in Torry,
bright and true and ringing.

A bleak day to cross the hill, traveller.
A shepherd with an eye-patch sees but half the
ewe-graving snow.

We are not innkeepers, traveller, and charge board.
Take this silver, Charon will have his due soon.

You must bide with us longer, seaman.
Cargo me with oil and bread, father, against the
troubling of the bar at sunset.

What do you seek at this door, traveller?
    The word is, you have good leaves for toothache.

Returns

There is no compulsion, those
Who've been made whole
Can chop logs beyond the burn.

Our garden has plenty of roots and stones
For hands renewed
If hands and hearts are willing, only.

An old patient can call in cow to byre.

If a man has ten gold pieces
He might leave one (scripturally)
That would build a new chamber of wholeness among the trees
If the forester is agreeable.

It is sufficient
To say *Ave* and *Gloria* in the hospice chapel.

from Don Juan, Canto the Tenth

George Gordon, Lord Bryon

As 'Auld Lang Syne' brings Scotland, one and all,
    Scotch plaids, Scotch snoods, the blue hills, and clear streams,
The Dee, the Don, Balgounie's Brig's *black wall*,
    All my boy feelings, all my gentler dreams
Of what I *then dreamt*, clothed in their own pall,
    Like Banquo's offspring; – floating past me seems
My childhood in this childishness of mine:
I care not – 't is a glimpse of *'Auld Lang Syne.'*

And though, as you remember, in a fit
    Of wrath and rhyme, when juvenile and curly,
I rail'd at Scots to show my wrath and wit,
    Which must be own'd was sensitive and surly,
Yet 't is in vain such sallies to permit,
    They cannot quench young feelings fresh and early:
I *'scotch'd*, not kill'd' the Scotchman in my blood,
And love the land of 'mountain and of flood.'

Byron's note: The Dee, the Don, Balgounie's Brig's *black wall* ... *The brig of Don, near the 'auld toun' of Aberdeen, with its one arch, and its black deep salmon-stream below, is in my memory as yesterday. I still remember, though perhaps I may misquote, the awful proverb which made me pause to cross it, and yet lean over it with childish delight, being an only son, at least by the mother's side. The saying as recollected by me was this, but I have never heard or seen it since I was nine years of age:*

    Brig of Balgounie, black's your wa',
    Wi a wife's ae son, and a mear's ae foal,
    Doun ye shall fa'!

George Gordon, Lord Byron (Aberdeen, 1924)
Marion Angus

This ae nicht, this ae nicht
By the saut sea faem,
The auld grey wife
O' the auld grey toon,
She's biddin' her bairns hame
Fae the far roads
An' the lang roads
An' the land that's ayont them a',
She's cryin' them hame
Till her ain toon
Atween the rivers twa.

This ae nicht, this ae nicht,
Fan the win' dra's fae the sea,
Thir's a laddie's step
On the cobbled steens –
Fatna laddie can it be?
Is't him that sang
Wi' the stars o' morn,
An' brak his her'rt
On a bleedin' thorn
An thocht nae mair o' me?

This ae nicht, this ae nicht,
the mirk an' the dawn atween,
Yon bairn he weers the Gordon plaid
An' his een's the eagle's een.
He sings as he gangs
By the Collidge Croon,
He fustles it ower the faem,
A queer auld rune

Til a gey auld tune,
I'm thinkin' my bairn's won hame.

For it's: *'Brig o' Balgownie,*
          Black's yer wa',
          Wi' a mither's ae son
          An' a mare's ae foal
          Doon ye sall fa'.'

Young Byron in Aberdeen

Alexander Scott

Thon hirplan bairn wi the face o a angel
Will sing like a lintie and loo like a deil,
He'll lowp out-ower convention's dreel
Tae connach the God o Calvin's evangel.

His tongue will teir frae reiver and strumpet
The laird's brocades and the leddy's braws,
Tae ding doun tyranny's Jericho waas
His miminy mou will rair like a trumpet.

The haulflins nou rin by him quicker,
Mockan, 'Ye're slaw eneuch for the grave!'
But he that yet will outrin the lave
Gangs hirplan forrart, slaw but siccar.

Brig o Balgownie

Sheena Blackhall

Brig o Blagownie, stoot's thy waa
The shaddas of heich trees doonfaa
Onno the wrunkled watter's broo
Roon banks lulled bi the Don's balloo.

Abeen its archwye, cauld an black
It cairries cobbles ower its back
Far traivellers dauchle, watchin dyeuks
In convey sail fur shady neuks.

Snaadrifts o clouds slide saft thegither
In archetypal simmer weather
For Don tynes its identity
In the braid quicksans o the sea.

Gates of St Machar Cathedral

Sheena Blackhall

I am standing in the queue waiting to die, quite near the front.
Not rushing, shuffling forward. Not anxious, neither impetuous
nor slow.
I shall not be sorry to go – I shall be nothing. The thought is quite
exciting.
I shall enter into the quiet mouth of the earth like a whisper.
So inviting

To slide below the soil, a weary sleeper,
Drawing the grave-mould covers above my head,
The fathomless void ... a black and a pleasant bed.
Folk say, there's no discourse amongst the dead.

I shall go like a fly to the waiting spider's lair,
I shall lay my hollow cheek by the winding worm,
I shall spill like an hourglass, breath turned empty air,
I shall be one with the yew and the granite urn.

Slowly the queue moves. Light gives way to black.
Nihil. The place where none come tell-tale back.

from The Brus

John Barbour

Thws in the hyllis levyt he,
Till the maist part off his menye
Wes rewyn, and rent; na schoyne thai had,
Bot as thai thaim off hydys mad.
Tharfore thai went till Abyrdeyne,
Quhar Nele the Bruyss come, and the queyn,
And othir ladyis fayr, and farand,
Ilkane for luff off thair husband;
That for leyle luff, and leawté,
Wald partenerys of thair paynys be.
Thai chesyt tyttar with thaim to ta
Angyr, and payn, na be thaim fra.
For luff is off sa mekill mycht,
That it all paynys makis lycht;
And mony tyme maiss tender wychtis
Off swilk strenthis, and swilk mychtis,
That thai may mekill pynys endur,
And forsakis nane auentur
That euyr may fall, with thi that thai
Thar throw succur thair liffys may.

Inscription at Fittie Kirkyard

Anon

George Davidson, elder, burgess, Abredonensis,
Bigit this dyk on his own expenses.

Folk

Epitaph from Aberdeen

Anon

Here lie the bones of Elizabeth Charlotte,
Born a virgin, died a harlot.
She was aye a virgin at seventeen,
A remarkable thing in Aberdeen

To an Aberdeen Poet Who Writes Solely in English

Helen B. Cruickshank

What ails ye at yer mither tongue?
Hae ye forgot the tang o' it?
The gurly guttrals, malmy soonds,
the dirly words, the sang o' it?
An wad ye cuist it a awa
Lik bauchles on a midden-heid?
Man, think agen afore ye sell
Yer saul to saft-lik English leid.

Wad ye forget the ballad-speik,
Melodeon's chord and fiddle's clink,
Forsweir yer grandad's ways o' life,
Swap usqueba for Kola drink?
Say 'Shinty is too tough a game
And cricket's more my cup of tea.'
Well hyne awa fae Aiberdeen
For feich, ye're owre genteel for me!

from A Drunk Man Looks at the Thistle

Hugh McDiarmid

Sae God retracts in endless stage
Through angel, devil, age on age,
Until at last his infinite natur'
Walks on earth a human cratur'
(Or less than human as to my een
The people are in Aiberdeen).

Cauld Kail in Aberdeen
Alexander, Duke of Gordon

There's cauld kail in Aberdeen
And castocks in Stra'bogie,
Where ilka man maun hae his lass
But I maun hae my cogie.
I maun hae my cogie, sirs,
I canna want my cogie;
I wadna gie the three-gir'd cog
For a' the queans in Bogie.

There's Johnnie Smith has got a wife,
Wha scrimps him o' his cogie;
If she were mine, upon my life,
I'd douk her in the Bogie.
I maun hae my cogie, sirs,
I canna want my cogie;
I wadna gie the three-gir'd cog
For a' the queans in Bogie.

Battle Sang o the Reid Army

Donald Gordon

For Aberdeen F. C. (Tune: 'The Church's One Foundation')

The fiery cross is glintin
On hielan hills afar.
The beacon fires are blinkin
On distant Lochnagar.
Fae Bellabeg tae Buckie,
The Broch tae Foggieloan,
The Granite Toon, an twal mile roon,
The reid battalions come.

Raise up the battle standard –
Oor flag is crimson reid.
An bravely i' the vanguard
It flees abune wir heid.
There's nane can staun afore us,
Sae gie's yir haun my frien,
Lat's sing the Victory Chorus –
The Sang o Aiberdeen!

All Clear in Aberdeen

Christine Laennec

'I was a WAAC,'
She told me sweetly.
Then: 'Do have a biscuit.'
Across the porcelain plate,
When I ask her please to tell me,
Her blue eyes open straight into mine.

'I was an air-raid warden
Up at Kittybrewster.
Oh the stars we had
In the blackout –
I wish you could have seen!
And the Northern Lights
Spread across the heavens
Night after night –
It was magical,
And so serene.

Of course there were bombs too
Falling from that same sky.
Once when morning finally dawned
I walked home over the Tarry Brig,
And every step was on shards of glass.
I didn't know
If I still had a home
To come back to ...'

The teapot she is holding
Quivers and stops in mid-air
Her eyes are focused
On a distance I cannot see;

Her hands are tense
With the memory of not knowing.

Then she snaps to attention
And finishes pouring.
'Well! It was still standing,
As you can see for yourself.
And oh what a welcome
We gave one another.
Won't you have a Viennese Whirl?
I do like a cup of tea
Of a forenoon.'

As I obligingly take another biscuit
I see
That only the gold pin at her throat
Is still shivering.

The Long Home

Robin Robertson

I hadn't been back in twenty years
and he was still here, by the fire
at the far end of the longest bar-counter
in Aberdeen – some say Scotland.
Not many in, and my favourite time:
the dog-watch; the city still working,
its tortoiseshell light just legible
in the smoked windows,
and through the slow delay of glass
the streetlights
batting into life.

The firewood's sap
buzzing like a trapped fly,
the granular crackle of a *Green Final*
folded and unfolded,
the sound of the coals
unwrapping themselves like sweets.
He only looked up when the barman
poured a bucketful of ice
into the sink, like a tremendous
burst of applause.

He was drinking Sweetheart Stout
and whisky, staring into the glass
of malt as if it were the past, occasionally
taking a pull on the long brown bottle.
I remember him telling me,
with that grim smile,
'I'm washing my wounds in alcohol.'
I liked a drink too,

but would always leave before him,
walking home, as if on a wire.

I'd heard what had happened
but wasn't ready for the terrible wig,
all down at one side, the turn
in his mouth and his face's
hectic blaze. He'd left here so bad
he could barely stand.
he'd got through his door, back to his room
and passed out for the night,
sleeping like a log with his head in the fire.

Patterns

Robin Munro

A thin line of logic holds Aberdeen
from the South, an invisible tripwire
you can break, but only once (like logic),
one hard and complete time.

You are on the ground,
the world's hatred stouning.

'There was a woman stabbit
yestreen in Aberdeen'
our simple man is telling me
'that never used tae happen.'

His line to the past is easy broken
for all the pattern was long in making.
I hear him trying to find a single strand, by day
I stumble through a night-time of it.

Trainie Park

Alastair Mackie

It wisna oor park, this green howe in the toun's hert
faur the track's causey rang and reekit
wi country trains and goods trains. Did the flooer-beds
get a skiftin o blawn brook the haill year roon?
A queer mixter-maxter thon –
reek and roses, stillness and the kink-hoast
o steam trains. Did auld men play dambrods there
ablow the granite dwaum o Robert Burns?
There we maun hae met and daffed wi quines or
rowed doun the grass braes ahin the gairdie's whussle …
Look up thonder to the main pend o the brig –
aneth it, trains cairriet fowk and lug-stoundin thunder –
aa Aiberdeen like black golochs gaun their eerands
dottit past, to win the Castlegate
Hizzelheid or the fower airts o the earth …

Victoria Park

Alastair Mackie

Le vert Paradis o Baudelaire? Never.
Already we kent ower muckle aboot quines ...
The gairdie was God, one-airmed, wi a whussle.

18th century parkland withoot a laird,
its graivel path began inside the gate,
– was it ever lockit? – a roosty carpet, trampin

to the fountain's weddin-cake, its tap a tree
upskailin watter that branched in smithereens.
We wyded in't and, ill-trickit Gullivers

we foonert boaties and splytert quines.
At Easter the eggs rowed. We climmed trees and yowled
like Tarzan or killt ane anither wi Woolie's guns.

Only the lovers, – we never saw them – dandert
thro Eden, nae yet yokey for God's aipple ...

Westburn Park

Alastair Mackie

Bradman o the centuries and Larwood
his richt hand, a cannon's snoot ... Whiles we had
a tree's knurly bole for wickets, whiles a tennis baa ...
I mind the simmer nichts the park's clock
was the clour and timmer yark o cricket bats
caain baas ower the grass and into the burn
and the batsman skirled on by his side, 'Rin, rin!'
We never had an umpire, the wicket-keeper
smoored the fast anes wi a jaiket. In the pond
the posh louns aired their yachts – nae Woolie's anes –
like white swans driftin wi their sails asleep ...
And the shaddas streekit their linth alang the grass
as we haiked doun Westburn Road, Jimmy Smith
singin, 'Throw open wide your window dear' ...

A City to Learn Love In

Aberdeen

Rachel Annand Taylor

Oh! that's a city to be born in.
   The pure air kindles you, and witty
Your mind goes dancing. To learn scorn in,
   Oh! that's a city.

The sea-birds cry wild things above, in
   The tender and the stainless sky.
Oh! that's a city to learn love in,
   Where sea-birds cry.

Under the Crown that dreams of Flodden
   And Borgia in scarlet gown
Youth lightly treads where Youth has trodden
   Under the Crown.

In Aberdeen, through years of splendour,
   You may ride mailed in gold and green.
Ironic folk to Youth are tender
   In Aberdeen.

The Brig o' Balgownie

Arthur Geddes

My luve sae lang, this day we'll gang
        ow'r the deeps o' the flowing Don,
Our tryst be the rig o' the ae-span Brig
        o' Balgownie ow'r the Don.

We'll win our way, dear lass, the day,
        where you turned to me, fain an' fon',
Seal troth at the Mairch where the poynted airch
        ow'rspans the darklin' Don.

Frae bank to bank sae steep and dank
        it rises til the sun:
Sae, groyne by groyne, our brig shall joyne
        baith banks till each be won!

Ye'll big wi' me, and I wi' thee,
        ae span, as ow'r the Don;
Lang twyned, we twain, our airch be ane
        though the river o' Time flow on.

At Melting Point

Eddie Gibbons

I am here and you are there.
Without you I am incomplete.
Perhaps the two of us should meet
at Melting Point in Golden Square.

I promise to be discreet.
You'll hardly even know I'm there.
You say you might as well stay where?
At Freezing Point on Silver Street?

Let's meet at the Lemon Tree.
Last year I overlooked you there.
Or where the poets meet upstairs –
at Books and Beans, if you are free.

Please sit at that window seat
I walked straight past this time last year.
Tonight I won't be late, I swear.
Where's Freezing Point on Silver Street?

I am here and you are there.
Without you I am incomplete.
Now one of us, at least, should meet
at Melting Point in Golden Square.

Roads in Rain

May C. Jenkins

We walk the rain-dulled roads
of Aberdeen;
our anger darkens love.

Milk-bottles clink
on steps;
doors open, shut.

People go hunched in the rain,
rushing last walks
with their dogs.

An occasional car leaps out
like a vast greyhound
from a side street.

'Why should we quarrel?'
you say,
taking my hand.

And grief is gone,
discarded in the streets;
a quiet comes.

Your touch is feather-soft –
but granite-strong –
dismissing rain.

Old Aberdeen

Jackie Kay

You'll never see what I'll give you
Out in the open country; the light coming in from the North Sea.
You'll never see what I'll give you
Up in the north, growing old under the lights of old Aberdeen.
You'll never see what I'll give you
A stone door opening to sunshine, the corn rigs the barley oh,
You'll never see, you'll never know
A song for every single day my love – Maxwellton braes are bonny.
You'll never see what I'd give you
Not now my lovely lassie oh.

The Bonnie Lass o' Bon-Accord

J. Scott Skinner

The Bonnie Lass o' Bon-Accord,
    Looks lang owre the bar o' the Dee,
An' the Bonnie Lass o' Bon-Accord
    Come's hame wi' the tear in her e'e.
An' there's never a wind but blaws to her gate
    Some brisk braw carle come to woo;
But wi' neither the kilt nor the coat will she mate,
    For her heart's wi' the jacket o' blue.

Her auld faither girns at the ingle side –
    'It's the Lowland squire ye maun wed,
An' ye to the kirk in a coach shall ride,
    An' in velvet an' silk ye'll be cled,
An' on siller ware ye shall dine at the board,
    An' the diamonds shall shine on your broo;'
But the Bonnie Lass o' Bon-Accord
    Still sighs for the jacket o' blue.

Her mither looks up frae her spinning wheel –
    'Ye maun lie on the bed that ye mak,
Ye're owre hard to please or your head's in a creel –
    It's the Hielant laird ye should tak',
Wi' his philabeg an' his lang broadsword,
    An' his kilt o' the scarlet hue,'
But the Bonnie Lass o' Bon Accord
    Sets her heart on the jacket o' blue.

Up speaks her sister, sae cankered an lean –
    'The menfolk are a' blin' or daft
To craze their heads for twa saucy een,
    An' a round face, silly an' saft;

But ye'll sink or swim if ye'll no tak' the ford,
   An' ye'll drink o' the browst that ye brew,'
An' there's mony a lass in Bon-Accord
   Cries – Rue on the jacket o' blue!

The Bonnie Lass o' Bon-Accord
   Turns round wi' the fire in her e'e –
'The carle, an' the clerk, an' the squire an' the lord,
   I wish they were droon'd in the Dee;
An' the siller hoard, an' the lang broadsword,
   An' the diamonds that shine on the broo –
Tak' them a' for ae blink frae Bon-Accord
   O' the ship wi' the jacket o' blue.

The Bonnie Lass o' Bon-Accord
   Gangs doon to the bar o' the Dee –
But the Bonnie Lass o' Bon-Accord
   Comes hame wi' the smile in her e'e –
An' she's missed at morn frae the bed an' the board,
   An' they harry the haill toon thro';
But the Bonnie Lass o' Bon-Accord
   Is aff wi' the jacket o' blue.

Alba: Aberdeen

Cate Marvin

A sky that blue is not a sad thing.
Some nights are not worth sleeping. And knowing
we'll never see a blue like that

ever again is fine. There are
nights not worthy of sleep. When the blue brims
like that and swallows the town

in its huge tear, the little
bridges we walk back over leave us. We're almost
back at your house, so we sit

in the alley and wait a while
for the sky to become normal. Our mouths marry
in smoke and the aftertaste

of Scotch. A man walks by
with his dog. Gulls shriek and dive; their noises
are terrible; the town wakes.

We pace some more before
returning each other's hands, then decide to sleep
the day. Your girlfriend is waking

for work. We are almost
asleep, in our separate rooms. Our lungs are blue
from breathing that color.

Our faces wear the same
expression. The sky is incapable of anything bluer.
Our hearts cannot be redder.

Watching the Menders

Wayne Price

Behind their George Street window,
ignoring the shoppers who all day
search for something new, the two
Lebanese tailors mend, bowed
at their benches, at their chattering
machines. Watching them, waiting again
for you, I could persuade myself
that watchers and watched all work
the same taut threads – between fingers,
between lips, in classrooms and pubs,
on pavements like this, on the pillows
of beds; so many invisible menders
of clothes that never fit or show

and anyway always tear. None of it
helps at all. I know that you, late again,
will soon not bother with these afternoons.
Everything happens once. You are
someone else; somewhere new.
For another last time I crane my neck
and one of the tailors lifts his head, turns
as if to meet my stare. His face is blank
behind the glass. The traffic crawls;
shoppers process like fish in a bowl. Both
emperor and boy in the tale were right,
dressed in their lonely question of what
nothing might be; how best to greet it.

Old Snapshot

George Bruce

The camera's shutter clicked. He'd caught
her for himself alone, he thought,
standing slim among the marguerites
against a sunny, summer wall with apples
on it. He put her in his pocket book in 1932.

The sepia mellows, seems to tell more true,
not just that moment long ago; collects
the happiness that walked through shady lanes
and by St Machar's towers at crook of Don
and through the Auld Toun's clattering streets,
bypassing the Bishop founder's tomb, to King's,
to sit amongst old words long dried on the page,
mountains of them, beautiful and boring,
wise and absurd – and still the moment breathes,
disturbs their dust.
                    Another place, another time,
from which she still looks out from that mute world
amongst the flowers, grown now most delicate.
And all the air of this dull day is changed.
Landscapes shout new with spring. Seas glitter
in their calm, and I, this breathing animal,
own such sweet strangeness as no words will do.

Low Pressure

Sue Vickerman

I said it would be stern as a school uniform,
dull as winter heather. But Aberdeen was gentle
as an egg box, pencil-shaded, hesitant outlines
smudged by the weather; cock-eyed sea-birds perched
on cardboard cut-out turrets high above the shops
on Union Street, while heads wrapped up like sweets
bobbed by, and men strode down to the gaudy ships

where you, delighted, took snaps of the docks,
metallic red and blue blocked into sketched space.
I could live here, you said, lingering at the sight
of a papery warehouse blown empty. That night
on the coast road we parked under lowering cloud
and argued, while behind us in fading light, the city
mulched like papier-mâché beneath the press of granite.

Grey Granite

Birthin Place

Joyce Everill

Weeds rantin ower an empty wame.
Forlorn. Forsaken noo the fame
that eence belanged tae it aleen.
The birthin place o'Aiberdeen.
Siller flecked, its very soul
yeildit tae the quarrier's tool.
Hewin, carvin, polish't gem
frae whaur this prood toon teen its name.
Causie setts an' monuments.
Braw mansions, halls an' tenements.
Grey Granite spewed frae oot its maw
tae big a city frae Rubislaw.

Granite Chip

Seamus Heaney

Houndstooth stone. Aberdeen of the mind.

Saying *An union in the cup I'll throw*
I have hurt my hand, pressing it hard around
this bit hammered off Joyce's Martello
Tower, this flecked insoluble brilliant

I keep but feel little in common with –
a kind of stone-age circumcising knife,
a Calvin edge in my complaisant pith.
Granite is jaggy, salty, punitive

and exacting. *Come to me,* it says
all you who labour and are burdened, I
will not refresh you. And it adds, *Seize*
the day. And, *You can take me or leave me.*

Aberdeen, the Granite City

George Bruce

The brown land behind, south and north
Dee and Don and east the doubtful sea,
The town secured by folk that warsled
With water, earth and stone; quarrying,
Shaping, smoothing their unforgiving stone,
Engineering to make this sufficient city
That takes the salt air for its own.
The pale blue winter sky, the spring green trees,
The castigating thunder rain, the wind
Beating about the midnight streets,
The hard morning sun make their change
By the white unaltered granite –
Streets of it, broad roadways, granite pavemented
To the tall tenements, rectangular wide-walled stores,
To the kirks and pillared Assembly Rooms;
Streets with drinking troughs for the animals,
And at the port quays crowded,
Overfed with horses, lorries, men and boys,
And always and at every point
Clatter on the causies.
Business is good, will be good here
At the dead end of time. Record then
This people who purposive and with strategy
Established a northern city, a coast town
That stands and stares by the waters,
Dee and Don and the sea.

Belmont Street

Thomas Rist

The men who built
This granite church
Had stony minds.
Their guilt was heavy
As the grey city
On graveyard days
And November's nocturne
Hung like blinds
On the lips of the lecturn.

Now where the grave men's
Hearts knelt down
They drink till they drown.
The young who dance
In the granite hall
Forget for all.

from Haunts: Aberdeen

Tim Tricker

The granite-silver in sunshine,
A brutal and bitter betrayal,
Beating senses senseless;
The grey-engrained betrothal,
A wearing steady strain,
The broken hearts of memory,
Placed, provided unkindly.

from Heart of Stone: A Poem on Aberdeen

Alexander Scott

The sea-gray toun, the stane-gray sea,
The cushat's croudle mells wi the sea-maw's skirl
Whaur baith gae skaichan fish-guts doun the quays
Or scrannan crumbs in cracks o the thrang causeys,
A lichthous plays the lamp-post owre a close,
The traffic clappers through a fishers' clachan
Whaur aa the vennels spulyie names frae the sea,
And kirks and crans clanjamfrie,
Heaven and haven mixter-maxtered heave
To the sweel o the same saut tide
Whaur aa the airts o the ocean anchor,
Ships frae the Baltic, ships frae Brazil,
Archangel ships wi a flag that dings archangels,
Coals frae Newcastle to thowe the cauldrife granite,
Planks that were aince an acre o Swedish wuids,
Esparto gress that greened in Spain,
And aye the sea's ain hairst o skinklan siller,
Haill flaughtered fleets o fish,
The sea-maws scraichan triumph owre their wreckage.
Nae wreckage haudden in hemmeran yairds
Whaur ships tak shape for the showdan shift o the sea,
Their cleedin steel, their steekin reid-het rivets,
They'll sclim frae their iron cradles
To fecht wi the iron faem and the stanie swaws,
Their strenthie sides as teuch as the sea-gray toun.

Druid Stone

John Sinclair

Wet,
in the city,
on the roof
of the night,
the Druid concrete
piles –
wait
for the sun
and its first
bloodstone cry
of mourning –
wait
in the hum
of the ring road
traffic
for the long day
of man's life –
wait
for the golden
scythe
on the towering flats
in a circle
round the
city
sacrifice.

Aberdeen Station

Harry Smart

You trek over granite setts
strewn with fragments of perspex, amber, red;
the broken teeth of heavy metal warriors shed
in slo-mo combats. Cigarette butts

are sown. If there's an apocalypse soon,
the silver city's sins come home to roost,
the broken teeth will sprout and shoot
new warriors up towards the bloody sun.

In the bar at the station the juke-box plays
a ballad; a stairway to heaven is provided
but the steps are steep, and they are guarded
by hellish stony-hearted beasties.

Computer Error: Neutron Strike

Edwin Morgan

No one was left to hear the long All Clear.
Hot wind swept through the streets of Aberdeen
and stirred the corpse-clogged harbour. Each machine,
each building, tank, car, college, crane, stood sheer
and clean but that a shred of skin, a hand,
a blackened child driven like tumbleweed
would give the lack of ruins leave to feed
on horrors we were slow to understand
but did. Boiling fish-floating seas slopped round
the unmanned rigs that flared into the night;
the videos ran on, sham death, sham love;
the air-conditioners kept steady sound.
An automatic foghorn, and its light,
warned out to none below, and none above.

Granite City Eclogue

Roderick Watson

Shines like frost   quartz hard   is worked with difficulty.
Perdurable.   A source of pride in character and action
is that glittering obduracy of mind   formidable
as Annie Davidson – a relative 16 years dead
and not far removed   who left service
as a lady's maid   by plaiting her employer's braids
into the back of the bedroom chair   and slapped her face
carefully   had six children (and five survived).
Her life's pride   was always to have managed.

But if endurance is a virtue   it makes us accomplice
to suffering   and its verity a convenient motto
for the merchant fathers who made more hose
out of less wool   by observing   what the girls wasted
at the end of the factory day   and stopping it.
For the men   who built grace into Grecian banks
and baronial hotels   and for the owners in their time
and elders of the steam trawler   in quiet houses
with sweet gardens   risen   from the fish
the stink of the catch   silver   on rusted plating
dredged out of the North Sea cold   blooded   teeming
the coin of that round and ruptured eye   bright as mica
exploding in the pan   brought in by the ton
on deck with frozen hands   split   raw   salt   flesh
weeks out for days in town   drinking   spending
sick as a cat in the lavvie – and out for more
two suits on the door   Sunday shoes under the bed.
For fish does not last   at all   and ripeness counts
and people have to manage   and damned if they don't.

Little virtue then   in such prideful exercise of grip
and scorn for what doesn't hold   and little ease
in the hard word.   Nevertheless   I value true things
by their difficulty   – a resistance to the will –
and celebrate this desperate intransigence   in all creation
for   at the last   I cannot credit grace
among accomplishments   in place of what is here and endures
nor deny the stern fathers   the merchant men
their inheritence   without accepting too
that ecstasy of opposition   which is how the son begins.

Defined by indirection   I am here
in the blossom of Cambridge   and away from home   mostly.

Black Gold

Return of the Tall Ships

G. A. McIntyre

In faded photographs:
'Aberdeen Harbour, eighteen-long-ago' –
    Each tapered mast a tree,
A floating forest of the tall old ships
Covers the water; they were graceful things,
    Lovely to see,
Their pyramidal rigging filled the air
Braced to endure the clear power of the wind
    On the wide sea.

And now the harbour holds
The first outriders of today's tall ships,
    The Glomars, Five and Three,
Heavy and dark, matching the new black fuel,
Great latticed pylons towering up once more
    Over the quay.
Another age, another style, but still
The same brave promise of prosperity
    From the wide sea.

Oilmen

Robin Munro

It wasn't the Springtime or the Autumn.
It was the winter that the strangers came
and offered money for our lives.

We are the people who were never fooled
or swung off balance like the others.
We saw through many a kilted boast.
We held back from the iron raiders.

I told them this, and I said –
you have no notion how they'll use us.
But their necks stretch to suck the sea,
their ears are full of the black
wealth chocking.

From all this, I make a song.
The power will always be the gold
and the barrel of the gun.
Poetry is the report
in whatever space is left.

In Aberdeen Library

Robin Munro

No, they do not
pay dollars for our women,
or, when broke, play
mean games with our children.

We, in turn, make
no creed of their helicopters
leading us to
Kingdom Come, laden like Woolworths.

(We hold a trace of an old faith;
the touble is –
while some make gods of mountains still,
the others dig.)

I'm wrong returning Melanesia
to the local section.
I agree with them, there is no good
connection, no, not really.

Boom Toon

Ken Morrice

The toon, boom city,
Houston o the North –
sombreros instead o bonnets?
black gowd instead o siller?

Havers! Frae Fittie
tae Rubislaw yer granite
waas'll halt sic an invasion.
The blunt speak o Aiberdonian
doddies winna encompass
yon obligatory drawl.

The smell onywey'll tell
ye. Nae ile – fish!

Old Torry

Ken Morrice

Timeless you might think, the huddle
of white cottages below the hill
leaning over wooden wharf – an ancestry
and heritage sure of our protection.

But history crumbles at the press of time.
And anyway it was all too personal,
too parochial. The boom of oil
calls louder than the cry of conservation.

Who listens to the fuss about tumbledown
old hovels? The jetty too looked dangerous.
Space was needed, steel and concrete
to moor the ships, support the storage tanks.

Yet when summer comes, I see again
the old kirk, the corner sweetie-shop,
the creaking yawls yawing at their ropes.
And at her door a fishwife busy

at her husband's lines, coiled and baited,
careful in their scull. But the cod
and haddock, the red-eyed mackerel,
swim deeper now. Pier looks bleak, empty

of raucous boys quarrelling over their catch
and teasing the gluttonous gulls
that swoop to swallow the wide world.

Not in stones now stands the fisher-town,
in memory only, in old men's minds.

East Coast: Aberdeen

Anne Stevenson

Old daughter with a rich future,
that's blueveined Aberdeen,
reeking of fish, breathing sea air
like atomized pewter. Her clean
gothic ribs rattle protests to the
spiky gusts. Pool girl.
She's got to marry oil.
Nobody who loves her wants to save her.

Cultural Revolution

Donald Gordon

As I gaed by the College Croon
I spied a braw-like carriage.
A denty lass wis steppin doon,
Aa buskit for her marriage.
Quo I: 'Ye tak a Buchan lad? –
For o but they are gallus!'
Quo she: 'You must be joking, Dad,
My luve wis born in Dallas!'

As I tae Turra did repair
I met this bricht young fella.
His breeks wis afa ticht, his hair
Wis different kinds o yella.
'Aye, aye,' quo I, 'Ye'll wint tae fee,
An see yir bairnies fed, man?'
Quo he: 'Corn rigs is nae for me.
It's ile rigs brings the bread, man!'

There's T-bone steaks in Aiberdeen,
Beefburgers in Stra'bogie.
Anither strike was made yestreen,
Sae bring alang yir cogie.
Ae day, they say, twil aa be ower,
Bit nae jist yet, by gum!
Half-owre, half-owre tae Aberdour
There's plenty still tae come.

Piper

George Gunn

For the 167 dead of the Piper 'Alpha'

My eyes are rivers of fire
& the dead feed on my chorus
on the smoke of a billowing column
on the applause of the bacon smellers
glad that they have not become
the plastic waft of melted hard hats
drifting over the gentle Summer sea
filled now with the black blood
of engineering & the fragile idolatry
of an unthought taking
        I see human tissue
turn to gas screaming its tune
of dolorous thanks through the twisted
rig legs & derrick girders flicked like pins
at the two handed dumbshow of finance & metal
& the dead sink in the neutral water
so many dead it is hardly bearable
they are at home now in the place of their origin
they fill my voice with their angry song
they sing
        'Fuck you, mate
fuck you' from under the feature pages
of middle-brow papers
list after list like nineteen fourteen
roughneck and roustabout, crane-op and cook
name after name in numbing insistence
singing
        'Back in Buchan the barley is turning
in Scotland now the Summer is green'
        My eyes see the hush-up shape & begin

from within Texan lawyers' attaché cases
it flies out, like a soul, at press conferences
like an invisible smog it both disappears & is seen
paving the way for back handed pay-offs
taking a loan of misery & grief
losing the place while we all watched
grown men confidently hoping that Red Adair
in his red asbestos longjohns
would ride out from the sunset
rewind the movie & make it OK
       This then the dream world of industrial oil
night after night it gets worse
the hush-up has swollen
to the size of Tehran
they park their Cadillacs in sinister places
& watch the sky burn like a torch
between the broken arms of the flare-off booms
holding the horizon still
for the many camera crews
so that we can all ooh & aah
feeling pity in our armchairs at the TV news
       I, a roughneck, tell you this
from the strange country of disbelief
the dead are always with us
we remember the dead

The Marginal Fields

Eddie Gibbons

The bottom's dropped out of the Barrel again,
and the gravy train has been derailed
at Aberdeen.

It's the downside of the fossil fuel boom,
the five-year lull when all the graphs
plunge off the page.

The Rigs are built to stand the *Hundred
Year Wave:* the surfer's wet wet dream.

But mortgages sink faster than gangsters
in concrete Reeboks, and here's me, mid-pool,
no snorkel in sight.

I've taken my leave of e-mails, Autocad,
bosses and tossers who think everyone else
is a wanker.

So it's back to the Doledrums;
the Onshore Survival Course:

stopped cheques, coffee mornings
with the bailiffs, Valentines
from the Procurator Fiscal,
Sheriff's Officers and the Hydro heavy gang.

I'm holding the fort until the markets
are buoyant and the Marginal Fields
surrender their yield.

Meanwhile, I've decided on the Writer's Life:
I'm translating Yevtushenko into Doric
and selling the texts at reserve games
at Pittodrie.

It's the job security that attracts me.

Scarlet Goon

Aberdeen University 1945–9

Iain Crichton Smith

I

The glitter of the water and the wake ...
Heading for University in Aberdeen.
It's an autumn morning. I am seventeen.
Above the Isle of Skye the dawn's a flag

of red infuriate ore. I see the train
for the first time ever steaming from the Kyle
beyond the screaming seagulls, in the smell
of salt and herring. There's a tall sad crane.

The landscape, rich, harmonious, unwinds
its perfect symmetry: not the barren stone
and vague frail fences I have always known.
I hold my Homer steady in my hand.

All day we travel and at last dismount
at the busy station of that sparkling town.
A beggar with black glasses sitting down
on the hard stone holds out his cap. I count

the pennies in it. Should I freely give?
Or being more shameful than himself refrain?
His definite shadow is the day's black stain.
How in such open weakness learn to live?

I turn away, the money in my hand,
profusely sweating, in that granite blaze.
Unknown, unlooked at, I pick up my case.
Everything's glittering and transient.

2

The prim historian talks of Robespierre.
Shakespeare's *Othello* is a mineral play
suited to granite and the wide North Sea.
Each subject has its scrupulous compère.

The guillotine cuts sharply between me
and that far island nesting in its waves.
Roof upon roof creates collapsing graves.
'Put up your bright swords.' Dewy Italy

and Aberdeen and Lewis all collide.
The sea-green incorruptible sustains
the sodden salty flesh. I shake my chains.
Europe is glowing like a flowery bride

with her fresh bouquets; and that ring recedes
mile upon mile away from me. I hear
the sharp quick yelp of tight-frocked Robespierre.
Some wound within me bleeds and bleeds and bleeds …

3

'Youse students with the cash,' says Mrs Gray,
our iron landlady with the Roman nose.
(Her stuttering husband is a paler ray.)

What art, what music, troubled even once
her brow that's wrinkled by the thought of gold?
She fills the space around her, holds her stance

against the world's obliquity. She stakes
her confident site out, while the scholar ghosts
through a double landscape of new streets, old Greeks,

a sturdy lady not to be put upon
by tragedy engendered in the soul,
nor by her husband who drives buses down

familiar roads, and who at night attends
religiously the 'flicks', whose bedroom is
the moony attic that her greed commends.

4
Beowulf dives into mysterious depths ...
The girls on Union St in cruising pairs
clutch shiny handbags, and wear Woolworth rings.

He swarms in armour towards an old death.
In Hazlehead their legs are white and bare.
They swim in twilight wafting vague soft scents.

His bubbling armour frays and leaks and dents ...
Their breasts at evening swell, their short skirts flare.
We are such fleshy fiery tenements.

The salty hero strides about his tents ...
My dear pale girls with permed and lamplit hair ...

5
Bicycles sparkle past the market place.
The cafés glitter. Love O Careless Love.
The statues cast their shadows across parks.

The velvet-jacketed pensioned Major moves
a piece on the draughtsboard in the open air.
This is a mimic and yet serious war.

I lie in Duthie Park with the *Aeneid*,
in my white flannels. All the epitaphs shine
in the adjacent overgrown graveyard.

LOVE O CARELESS LOVE. The Odeon towers
in its white marble towards a blue decor.
Its transient images are what etch and burn.

And in the café a small radio plays.
Everything passes, everything is weighed
with a random music, heartbreakingly sweet.

6
Aberdeen, I constantly invoke
your geometry of roses.

Your beads of salt
decorate my wrists

and are the tiny bells
of grammar schools.

There are no deaths
that I recall

among your cinemas,
in the shadows

of your green trees.
Aberdeen,

I loved your granite
your salt mica.

Your light
taught
me immortality.

7
No library that I haven't loved.
My food is books.

The grey-haired twittering lady climbs the steps
to drag a heavy Spenser to the floor.

She is not made of crystal but is mortal.
An old professor is bent over a chair
drowsing perhaps sleeping.

How reconcile
the market to the library, the till
to strict Lucretius?

The foam of flowers in Duthie Park, the page
blazing in its whiteness, in this sun
whose sleepless socket is perpetual.

The grey-haired lady lugs a tome across
a library floor as polished as a glass.

O she will die but this book will never die.
The Faerie Queene; this pale dishevelled one.

8
In winter, ice and frosty Aberdeen
inscribes its images on window panes.

The Polar Star is miles away from us.
It glows on towers and ghostly lighthouses
and on the spiky Latin in my room.

This is your weather, strict Lucretius.
How can religion stand it? How can Pan
with his hairy tropic legs? That animal?

The frost an exhalation of the mind.
The icy planets keep their rectitude.
Religion dies in temperatures like these.

And God the spider shrinks in his crystal web.
The gravestones bloom with ice. The city is
a constant shrine of probabilities.

The King's Student

Olive Fraser

All men do sleep in night and darkness dead
Save thee, Callimachus, reading in bed.
Thy windy candle lights a page, a part,
But a great, crownéd lantern lights thy heart.

A Scarlet Goon

Jessie Kesson

O the regret as a body growes auld!
I wad hae likit a scarlet goon
an' a desk o' my ain 'neath the auld, grey Croon.
But I nivir wun nearer the College airts
than a Sunday walk doon the cobbled toon.
King's gaithered a' its ain wise thochts
intae its ain grey fauld.
Bein' young, I grippit on tae the daftest thocht of a',
feel, feckless, wi' naething to ponder on
but a tryst tae be keepit by Brig o'Don.
Gin I'd hae worn a scarlet goon
Fat wad I ken?
Mair or less than I ken noo
livin' mang men wha nivir heard o'
Aristotle, or Boyle, that made a law,
or Pythagoras, an' sic like chields
wha's wisdom's gie heich up, and far awa'.
My Alma Mater's jist the size o' a' the fowk I ken,
An' jist the colour o' their thochts,
grey whiles wi' mole-hill griefs that mak true mountains;
gowd harled wi' sma' lauchs and greater humour;
black wi' humphy-backed despair;
alowe wi' hopes that whiles come true
but mair than often find slow beerial there.
And whiles it's green,
For jealousy torments even lads
wi' nae letters ahint their names.
A' that I ken.
– But still, I'd hae likit a scarlet goon,
an' a desk o' my ain 'neath the auld grey Croon,
Learnin' a little from the wise.
Dauncin wi' gowden sheen,
Lauchin' wi care-free eyes,
– Instead o' lifting tatties in mornin's glaured and cauld.
– O the regret, as a body growes old!

The Professor's Wife

Flora Garry

I wis a student at King's.
Ma folk hid a craft in Glenardle.
'Learnin's the thing,' they wid say,
'To help ye up in the wardle.'

They vrocht fae daylicht to dark.
Fine div I min' on ma midder,
Up ower the queets amo dubs,
Furth in the weetiest widder.

Swypin the greep in the byre,
Forkin the crap on the laan,
Treetlin wi water an aess an peats,
Aye a pail in her haan.

I wis a student at King's.
O the craft I nivver spoke.
Peer and prood wis I
An affrontit o ma folk.

An fyles on a stull Mey nicht
I wid tak a daaner roun
By Spital and College Bounds
To the lythe o the Aal Toon.

An I wid stan an glower
In at the windows wide
O the muckle hooses there
Far the professors bide.

At cannle-licht an flooers
Shinin silver an lace,
An, braw in a low-neckit goon,
The professor's wife at her place.

'Fine,' says I to masel,
'Fine to be up in the wardle,'
An thocht wi a groo, on the brookie pots
In the kitchen at Glenardle.

'Learnin's the thing,' says I,
'To help ye up in the wardle.'
I wed a professor come time
An gid hyne awaa fae Glenardle.

I bide in a muckle dark hoose
In a toon that's muckle an' dark,
An it taks me maist o the day
To get fordalt wi ma wark.

Traachlin wi sitt an styoo.
Queuein for maet for oors,
A body his little time or hert
For cannle-licht an flooers.

Ma hans are scorie-hornt,
An fyles I fin masel
Skushlin ma feet, as ma midder did
Oot teemin the orra pail.

The aal folk's lyin quaet
In the kirkyard at Glenardle.
It's as weel; they'd be gey sair-made
At the state noo-a-days o the wardle.

'Learnin's the thing,' they wid say,
'To gie ye a hyste up in life.'
I wis eence a student at King's.
Noo I'm jist a professor's wife.

from Marischal College

Ronald Campbell MacFie

Eternity was author of thy plan;
The fire-mist, and the sun and earth, and man
Joined in the making. Yea, by fire and thought
The gracious granite miracle was wrought.
And now thou art full-grown –
Full-leaved, full-blown –
An encrinite,
Stately and white,
A lily made of stone –
A torch that flares across the night
Of the Unknown –
The spindle and the loom of light –
An altar and a throne –
A temple where the feet of Truth may fare –
A peak where wisdom may be set on high,
Under a cloudless sky,
In Alpine air.

The Well at King's

Sheena Blackhall

I am the well. Hang your face over me.
Let me be the drum stick to your tabor,
Let me fill an empty moment with delight.
My shadow-theatre ripples with quicksilver,
Sundial silhouettes. The seasons pirouette along my sides
No wind disturbs my mole-ish, tunnelled chamber.

I am the well, a catacomb of moons.
Dropped stars shine on my surface like doubloons.
I wear black mourning bands along my wall.
Each century that passes, leaves its mark.
I seep from rock's cupped hand,
A fresh stigmata, ever-open wound.
My waves are dragon's scales
That shimmer in the netherland of dark.

Visit me. Be a shard of my mosaic.
A water-colour sky, stipples my brow with rain,
I sieve it down like ghostly seeds of grain.
I swallow it. My mouth is a dark stain.
Rain's generations drown in my domain.

Winter shuts my eye with rheumy frost
Blinds me with a cloudy, icy lid. Autumn's disc is slate.
Summer's shining plate's aquamarine.
My retina's an ever-changing scene,
Where flapping wings of birds
Speed past to unknown destinations.
I am a moored watcher. No cataract, no great Ulyssean ocean,
A litmus paper puddle of stagnation.

I am the sole sphere, in the square quad,
Quiescent cell of quiet resignation.
I am a tethered meeting place, a tryst.
The essence of my gold-fish bowl directive
Is simple ... entertain all pausing guests,
A Cyclops with a periscope perspective

I am a pit of wishes, pot of dreams,
Tossed money, on the spun roulette of hope
Escapism … day dreaming, drink, or dope,
Relaxes each tugged puppet, on its rope.
Coins thud like arrows striking dead on target,
I quiver at the point of penetration.
Concentric wheels fly out, like spinning rings.
I am the stuff of magic, myth, and hype
I am forever, a deep archetype.
I am a transient tableau, fluid tapestry,
A wobbly outline of a stranger's stare,
The soft white underbelly of a chin,
Shudder of lip, of nostril, wavy flow of hair
Are bit parts on my queer, unscripted screen,
A moment'ry addition to my lair.
I am an amputated ancient function.
The slit veins of my bucket,
Cut me adrift from life. My alienation
Was complete and planned. No hand
Now lifts my dripping, brimming treasure.
Contextual ties are severed. I am become a fossil,
A rusty medal from a mildewed war.
Only the dusk drops into my cold womb.
The fastidious, seditious, the malicious,
The credulous, the clever, as they pass,
May stop, to drop their likeness in my glass.
I turn each gold Narcissus into brass.
Listen … put your ear against my side
I capture echoes, layers of muted sound …
The hollow hoot of the owl, the peal of bells,
Shuffle of footsteps, muffled human speech,
Things shouted, whispered, all sink underground.
I resurrect them, sometimes, to confound
The daylight passers by, who may forget
Nothing escapes the web of memory's net.
Heavens may vastly wheel their cosmic course,
I need no angels, I am my own halo.
I shall be here, when masonry has tumbled
I spring eternal from my secret source.

Return to Aberdeen University

Iain Crichton Smith

Thirty six years afterwards I return.
Everyone's so young. The days of iron
soften intently towards my youth again,

when I was one of those who sparked my wit
in loose cheap blazer along Union Street
and the moony chimes struck heavily through the night.

So young, so young! The cinemas are gone,
replaced by bingo. The theatre remains
refurbished in gold leaf and Cupid wings.

Remember me. I strolled in Hazlehead
when the autumn leaves were golden overhead
and girls with cracked handbags giggled down the street.

The statues were imperious, overblown.
In bare religious Lewis there were none,
only the justice of the windswept stone.

Bookshops and churches, buses, study rooms.
There is a play of wavering white flames.
We have lived since then through the most violent times,

but the quadrangles remain quiet as once before.
I push (extraordinarily) this well-known door.
I am an explorer, but what I explore

is the past not present. The professors change,
the lecturers are bearded, young and strange.
At fifty seven to casually range

the roads of yesterday seems eerie now.
Time eats us momently. Paunchy, middle brow,
how can I face the idealist I knew

intense, self-conscious. Or how justify
the choices and the failures? Oh, we die
so many times, on our concessive journey.

This is a resurrection and a death.
Pale ghost, I love you, but your venomous breath
would kill me now, I think. Not all the earth

is possible imperium, I say.
I am the Roman of another day
the gaunter copy of a vast Idea,

Platonic and autumnal. Let me live.
Do not condemn me to another grave
but take me by the hand. O please forgive

your elder and your senior. Be polite.
Open the doors for me. Give up your seat,
my blazing adolescent. Don't repeat

old jokes about me. Do not mock or scorn.
You also had your days of smoke and iron.
You also had a life (not book) to learn

and saw the leaves deceive you, become frayed.
You also were by marble speech betrayed,
the adamantine proverbs of the dead.

So let us walk together down this street,
a father and a son perhaps, in light
of supernatural clarity and granite

sparkling with a memory and a present fire.
The cobblestones are shaky. O for fear
that we fail or falter let us walk together

in the common merciful air so bright and green
in ancient solid vanishing Aberdeen.

Outwith

Rostov-on-Don (1942)

Flora Garry

The Mountains of the Caucasus
Invest that foreign sky.
Under the bridge-heads of that Don
Men, dead, go floating by.

Bell heather blooms on Bennachie
Red this bright summer day
And down by Inverurie town
Men work among the hay.

Why should I thole this alien woe,
For duly unkent repine?
The flower of war incarnadines
Another Don than mine.

Chicago Aberdeen Arbroath

Donald MacEwan

It was odd that Aberdeen should enter
His thoughts then, incongruous as the precentor
Watching *Top of the Pops*, as the sirens
Wailed down Erie and environs,
Oblivious to Britain's number one
And the Free Kirk; and to the sun
Mooching his way westward over Scotland,
Observing a hundred coffee mornings (What land
Does not claim her sun as her own?) But it did,
Odd though it was. Below him, the grid
Stretched out like an infinite cushion south,
Till the lights merged into a fuzzy mouth
Whispering neon sweet nothings through the clinging,
Sour, breathless, hot, singing
Broth. He chuckled over the ignorant city,
Thinking of an old story which Aunt Kitty
Knew, about the man who asked if Granny
Was in; 'I'm sorry,' he was told. 'Ye cannae
See her – she's at Arbroath.' 'That's fine,'
He said, 'I'll wait till she's feenished.' The line
Giggled down Madison, and in downtown Big Macs,
Cackled in China town and sleepless fax
Machines, laughing with intimate friends
In New York Paris London, ends
Of the Earth, Moscow, Tokyo, Aberdeen:
The newest stop on the global scene
For oil and herring. The thought was so daft
That the couple below looked up as he laughed
Till he cried and cried, but with more sorrow
Than mirth in the tears tumbling into to-morrow
Where was home in this city? laid bare

Like a centrefold before him, yet greyer
And more inscrutable than a fishwife
Looking East; a crawling still life
with 'WET PAINT' scrawled on the sidewalk.
He dare not touch …
                              He woke with a shock.
Light blared insolently past his head
Bleary with dried tears. Quietly he shed
His clothes, unwilling to wake any more,
Wrapped a towel round, and closed the door
Softly behind, moving toward the shower room.
As the water spattered down warm, he wondered whom
He'd meet to-day: preachers speaking
Of your soul and alcohol; buskers seeking
Pennies from businesspeople deep
In conference and a tuna sub, and a heap
Of kids rolling past crosslegged blind, their upturned
Hats full of Coca-Cola cans spurned
By the good and evil alike. There was no home
In this city, but the people and the streets to roam,
And Aberdeen entered his thoughts again
As he scuffed his way East at ten after ten.

John Imlah

Mick Imlah

'The Hermit, ... placing before the Saracen a pitcher of sherbert, assigned to the Scot a flask of wine.' – The Talisman

He never left his native Aberdeen,
Where the triple rivers rin sae clear and fresh;
But since he bore the alcoholic gene,
Better if he'd been born in Marrakesh.

Aberdeen

Hazel Hutchison

Aberdeen
is just like Venice
apart from the cars
and the lack of canals
and the absence of Tintoretto
and the fact that we have no opera house
and the buildings are grey
and the people are pale
and tourists don't cluster on bridges in spring
like blossoms on a bough –

but other than that.

There are places in the world
where the past seeps up through the stones like a tide
and the grid of the old lies visible
under the line of the new
and the tang of the undrained salt-marsh of history
hangs in the air, immediate, restless

and we eat pickled herring
and honour the violin
and spend a lot of money on designer clothes
and we build fewer boats

and yesterday over the low-slung roofs of King Street
hung a perfect Canaletto sky.

Lang Journey Back

Donald Gordon

I'm scunnert wi the lotus days
An trauchled wi the heat
An I think on a land abune the win
Faur the day is roch an weet:
Faur the wild geese cry in a gurlie sky
An the rain is sweet.

I mind me yet on a hard, thrawn land
Wi eident fowk forbye
An a gangrel loon in an auld gray toon
Anaith a norlan sky
Awa i' the mists at the edge o the warld
Faur the great gulls cry.

Mirk the nicht, wi flauchts of fire
Faur the lift is aa aflame.
On the win that blaws i' the hollow hills
Ye can taste the saut sea faem:
An I hear the roarin o the sea
As I tak the low road hame.

Bus Journey Home

Dorothy Henderson

Home travelling home, like a pigeon to dove-cot
Sniffing the keen breeze that wafts from the sea,
Breath-taking glimpse of the fay town of Gourdon,
Harbour and rocks, frothing waves running free.
On we go on past soft sweep of pale harvest field,
Yellow and shining, the stubble blades gleam
Caught by the sunlight, left by the garnered yield,
Proud and accomplished, with satin-smooth sheen.
Dunnottar, its noble walls huddled, lies dreaming,
Bungalows, cottages, cattle sweep by,
Barley fields waiting the harvester's gleaning
Stretch in their glory, and climb to the sky.

Potato fields, shaw-burnt, wait for the lifting,
Mayweed and mustard with poppies glow bright.
There hovers a kestrel, with pointed wings quivering,
Expectantly poised, then hid from my sight.
But home, I am home, with the rupture still clinging,
Crossing again our dear River Dee,
Back to the heart of the grey Granite City,
Sparkle of sunshine on house, spire and tree,
Plaint of the herring gull, circling the trawler fleet,
Cold salt tang of our Aberdeen sea.

Aberdeenshire

Robert Crawford

Oilrig excaliburs of burning gas,
Sheep coughing through a starlit igloo silence
Near Craigievar, the reeling of dancers

Spattering an on-off wind's signal
Broken up by granite and salmon,
Whitewater *bon viveurs*.

The King's College corona satellite-tracks
Star dialects. Hills budge
And settle. Grouse flurry. Computer screens dazzle the night,
Their flickering eyes added to the land's.

All Seasons

Aberdeen Seasons: Four Haiku

Alan Spence

sudden gust –
the seagull scudding
backwards

midsummer midnight
full moon in the pale sky
over the north sea

the oystercatcher's cry –
cold loneliness,
the far north

chant from the mosque –
there is one god, allah …
cold aberdeen night

Butterfly in the Shiprow

G. A. McIntyre

Old, round, pale-orange stones, warm in the sun,
Nettles, a ragged splash of green, hard by,
And on the green a fiery butterfly,
A vivid sparkle in that dusty street.
It might be small enough surpise to meet
A Painted Lady there, and scarcely more
The odd Red Admiral, so near the shore,
Zig-zagging into town in search of fun.
      This was a Tortoiseshell, its wings outspread.
      Blue-fringed, black and white spotted, orange-red,
      It spiralled up, past vision, and away,
      Leaving the street below suddenly dead;
      It's ill for butterfly – or man – to stay
      Among stone walls on such a summer day.

Aberdeenshire Elegy

Peter Davidson

Amor Patriae, epistle to CDR

Smoke over conifers, rumours of snow in October
Corgarff under frost; the Spey running broad over stone
(The rowans going over to gold, the first larch branches tarnishing)
Last slant of summer now passing, now past, in reaped meadows
    under our towers.

Soft dust on the fields now, showing white towards harvest,
Haar over barley, days closing in, summer boats anchored in harbour,
Leaving us lonely below cloud roads of flocks moving southwards
Awaiting the first real breath of cold from the mountains,
Alone with our north, husbanding this difficult land.

Austere virtuosi of absences, distance, occlusions,
Collectors of outland colours: dun, bistre, gradations of grey,
Salt-scatter of snow on the marl and ash of the ploughlands.
Bare trees lustred only at sunset in scarlet, frost-sapphire and azure –
The west limned with glimpses into bright realms in the hills.

Connoisseurs too of the north in its sombre closet of wonders:
Latin scratched on glass against early-westering light,
Treason glasses blowing lost midwinter roses,
Glass negatives of spires misted by time and the winter,
The spiral horn keeping the door of the chamber of twilight and ice.

So we look down from the Shiprow to icebreakers waiting their
    hours of departure
For norths barely imagined: white drift in brilliant night.
And think on our frontier Dukedom, rubble altars marking bounds
    of the Empire.
Last, remotest throw of the Romans: cold cairns on the horns of Ross
Stone portals of absolute north, farthest obelisks of snow.

Aberdeen Train

Edwin Morgan

Rubbing a glistening circle
on the steamed-up window I framed
a pheasant in a field of mist.
The sun was a great red thing somewhere low,
struggling with the milky scene. In the furrows
a piece of glass winked into life,
hypnotized the silly dandy; we
hooted past him with his head cocked,
contemplating a bottle-end.
And this was the last of October,
a Chinese moment in the Mearns.

Aberdeen: A Poem in Autumn

Gerard Rochford

It is a good month for shedding poems.

Leaves have piled high in the books of the dead.
The occasional flush of a Virginia Creeper
stirs unvirginal lust in this ashen city.
And when we sleep in beds of roses
night-mares graze, their mouths red with petal.

Beyond the city we have destroyed the forest
and posted troops of Pine to guard the streets
where paper grows.
Even my love lies to attention
in those disciplined woods.

Texan drills, launched from the harbour,
shaft upon the sea-bed,
breaking it with astonishing harvest.
Dollars, shaped like a friendly sea-horse,
drive the fish from square allocations of water.

Fishermen, expecting silver,
trawl nets plump with death.

Our gulls climb now laden with danger.
Send them to me to land in my fishless garden,
where they may walk like pensioners on wide feet,
paddling across daisies,
fussed over by brash starlings
and the sweet branches of Lime.

And when uneasy skies stir them to flight,
I will love their porcelain bodies,

help them to forget the wind's horizon,
protect them from waves weary with oil,
despairing of gifts from these once easy seas.

This Autumn, my city and its trees are neat with loss.

Lean Street

G. S. Fraser

Here, where the baby paddles in the gutter,
    Here in the slaty greyness and the gas,
Here, where the women wear dark shawls and mutter
    A hasty word as other women pass,

Telling the secret, telling, clucking and tutting,
    Sighing, or saying that it served her right,
The bitch! – the words and weather both are cutting
    In Causewayend, on this November night.

At pavement's end and in the slaty weather
    I stare with glazing eyes at meagre stone,
Rain and the gas are sputtering together
    A dreary tune! O leave my heart alone,

O leave my heart alone, I tell my sorrows,
    For I will soothe you in a softer bed
And I will numb your grief with fat to-morrows
    Who break your milk teeth on this stony bread!

They do not hear. Thought stings me like an adder,
    A doorway's sagging plumb-line squints at me,
The fat sky gurgles like a swollen bladder
    With the foul rain that rains on poverty.

Home Town Elegy

G. S. Fraser

For Aberdeen in Spring

Glitter of mica at the windy corners,
Tar in the nostrils, under blue lamps budding
Like bubbles of glass the blue buds of a tree,
Night-shining shopfronts, or the sleek sun flooding
The broad abundant dying sprawl of the Dee:
For these and for their like my thoughts are mourners
That yet shall stand, though I come home no more,
Gas-works, white ballroom, and the red brick baths
And salmon nets along a mile of shore,
Or beyond the municipal-golf course, the moorland paths
And the country lying quiet and full of farms.
This is the shape of a land that outlasts a strategy
And is not to be taken with rhetoric or arms.
Or my own room, with a dozen books on the bed
(Too late, still musing what I mused, I lie
And read too lovingly what I have read),
Brantome, Spinoza, Yeats, the bawdy and wise,
Continuing their interminable debate,
With no conclusion, they conclude too late,
When their wisdom has fallen like a grey pall on my eyes.
Syne we maun part, their sall be nane remeid –
Unless my country is my pride, indeed,
Or I can make my town that homely fame
That Byron has, from boys in Carden Place,
Struggling home with books to midday dinner,
For whom he is not the romantic sinner,
The careless writer, the tormented face,
The hectoring bully or the noble fool,
But, just like Gordon or like Keith, a name:
A tall, proud statue at the Grammar School.

Geoffrey A. Oelsner
Song for Aberdeen

Aberdeen,
    I will remember
your moth-gray granite streets
    daubed with yellow daffodils,
the angel in your pubs
    playing accordion,
tall ships
    rigged with mist
in your dawn harbor.
    Aberdeen,
King's College saturated
    with thought,
tier upon tier of leather bound volumes,
    the cobblestone river
shining in noon light,
    I will remember.
There is a circular hill
    above Seaton Park,
above the humming mills by the Don,
    where I first heard your song
blow seaward on a soughing gull-wind,
    Aberdeen.
It was song
    that welled from granite
darkness heavy and black
    as galactic space;
exploded forth as the green crowns
    of trees in Spring.
There were sounds of people:
    singing, fighting,

pivoting from pain to sleep
    to morning hope.
The woman in her shop
    selling pastries,
school children subverted
    by sun and giggles
from Latin,
    the bus conductor's
'Both sides now,'
    the paper seller shouting
evening's gospel from his corner pulpit
    (Amazing Full-Page Picture) –
all these interwove
    and the chorus blew by.
It passed through bent beach-grasses
    and was drawn into the sea's roar.
So it has been
    since before Elphinstone,
before St Machar's,
    before even the oldest
rain-beaten gravestones.
    Since the first settlers
laid stone upon stone,
    lit fire in hearth,
spoke together in a tongue
    closer to the wind's syntax
than our own,
    the sea,
that swaying darkness,
    has taken all your songs.
But you have drawn
    from her;
made silver from the glistening

scaled silver in the nets,
suffering wind-lash and rope-burn
 to do this.
The voices of sailors lost at sea
 ring up like vertigo.
I hear faint cries
 as your ships plough eastward,
Aberdeen.
 They are not from gulls.
Outside the city,
 gunmetal gray combers
drive in toward shore.
 Twilight.
The sun casts
 strange Angelus light
that limns the fence-wires
 and barn roofs;
infuses the hushed earth.
 Looking to your foundries
with their great fists of smoke
 clenched above the city,
looking to the cage of lights
 blinking on,
I know I will remember you as a home,
 Aberdeen.
Smoky conversations, an archive
 of faces circle in my memory.
Not the memories, however,
 but the moments themselves
are the value,
 so while I am here
I add my voice
 to your sea-bound song,
Aberdeen.

from The Dream and the Deed

George Rowntree Harvey

I love this place, all seasons of the year:
Men of the south who do not know its charm
Think of our northern Aberdeen as only
A tent of skies that has its differing shades
Of grey; as a haunt of snow and rain, of winds
As snell – little they know, who do not live
Upon our seven hills and taste the changing sweets
Of every season here. No other place
I've seen sees autumn come with richer gold,
With lovelier tapestries at dawn or set
Of sun. Often it seems to me our autumn
Is but the birth of spring; thoughts of decay
Can never flourish in this seaward place.
The leaves may fall, the fields be bare, but then
The Don, the Dee grow stronger, swiftlier flow
To meet the sea that has no fading time.

Glossary

aess   ashes
alowe   ablaze
bauchle   worn out old shoe
beriall   beryl, precious stone
bleedy doctors   sticklebacks
big   build, make
brook   soot
browderit   embroidered
buskit   dressed, prepared
bygyne   building
castocks   cabbage stocks
causey   causeway
cassies   cobblestones
clanjamfrie   crowd together
clour   hit, dent
cogie   drinking cup
connach   waste, spoil
crans   measures of fish
croce   cross
croudle   cower, nestle
cruke   lameness
cushat   wood pigeon
daffed   fooled, flirted
dambrods   draughts
dauchle   dander, tarry
dirdcd   bumped
ding   hit, beat
dirly   throbbing, thrilling
doddie   hornless cow or sheep,
    person
dottit   hurried, staggered
dowie   nostalgic
dyeuks   ducks
dwaum   day-dream
eident   diligent
encrinite   a fossil crinoid

fain   loving, affectionate
feel   daft
flauchts   flares
foonds   foundations
foonert   foundered, capsized
fordalt   well ahead
gannand   wandering
gert   ordered
girds   metal hoops
girned   whined
glaured   muddied
golochs   beetles
gowd   gold
greep   gangway
groo   shudder
gurlie   threatening, stormy
haar   coastal fog
heich   high
hirple   limp
hoasts   coughs
howk   dig
jow   ring
kink-hoast   whooping cough
kist   chest, box
lave   rest, remainder
lift   sky
lintie   linnet
loo   love
louns   lads
lug-stoundin   ear-numbing
mauna   will not
midden-heid   rubbish dump
mools   graveyard earth
mowdies   moles
mystere   dream
orra pail   slop pail

pend arch
philabeg kilt
preclair distinguished
queets ankles
quines lasses
remeid remedy
roy prince, sovereign
runklet wrinkled
sclim climb
scrannan scrounging
scud a blow with a belt or tawse
seg seat
showdan rocking
siccar secure
skaichan scrounging
skail scatter, disperse
skinklan sparkling
skushlin shuffling
smirr drizzle
snell sharp, biting
snochert snorted
splytert splashed

sted site
stour conflict
sturt strife
styoo dust
swaws waves
teemin emptying, pouring
teuch tough
three-gir'd cog cup with three
     metal bands
thole endure
timmer wooden, timber
trauchled troubled, laboured
treetling trotting
unkent unknown
usqueba whisky
vrocht worked
wame, wyme womb
wardle world
warsled wrestled
werd fate
yark thud
yokey restless

Biographical notes

Alexander, Duke of Gordon (1743–1827) was the fourth Duke of Gordon, inheriting the title and the family estate at Huntly at the age of nine. A loyalist, like his father, he raised a regiment for the British government during the American War of Independence. He became a Knight of the Order of the Thistle in 1775. He was a friend of Robert Burns, who is said to have admired his poems and songs. Gordon was elected the Chancellor of the University of Aberdeen in 1793. He is buried in Elgin Cathedral.

Marion Angus (1865–1946) was born in Sunderland the eldest of eight children, and moved with her family to Arbroath when she was eleven. She began writing journalism for the *Arbroath Guide*, but after her father's death in 1902 she moved with her sister to Aberdeen, where she lived for most of the rest of her life, teaching and writing. Her first publication of poetry was *The Lilt and Other Verses* (1922), followed by five further volumes. She had a lively personality and forthright views, but did not marry. She died in Arbroath in 1946.

John Barbour (c. 1320–95) known as 'the father of Scottish poetry' was the Archdeacon of Aberdeen, during the early phases of the building of St Machar's Cathedral. Although little is known about his personal life, Barbour travelled widely, receiving several passports to journey to Oxford and Paris for study, and he later served as auditor in the household of King Robert the Second. In 1378, the King granted him a pension to be paid from the revenues of the Burgh of Aberdeen, probably in recognition of the completion of his epic poem *The Brus*.

Meg Bateman was born in Edinburgh in 1959 and attended the University of Aberdeen from 1983 to 1990, and subsequently taught there from 1991 to 1998. She lectures at Sabhal Mòr Ostaig in Skye. She has translated three anthologies of Gaelic material for Birlinn and has published three poetry collections. *Aotromachd / Lightness* (1997) and *Soirbheas / Fair Wind* (2007) were both short-listed for the Scottish Book of the Year.

Sheena Blackhall is a writer, illustrator, traditional ballad singer and storyteller in North-East Scotland. From 1998 to 2003 she was Creative Writing Fellow in Scots at the Elphinstone Institute at the University of Aberdeen. She has published four novellas, ten short-story collections and over sixty poetry collections. Two of her plays have been televised. She has won several national awards for Scots poetry and short-story writing.

George Mackay Brown (1921–96) was born in Stromness, and spent most of his life in the Orkney Islands, apart from the years he spent studying at Newbattle Abbey College and the University of Edinburgh. Throughout his life, Mackay

Brown was dogged by ill health, especially pulmonary tuberculosis, which forced him to have several extended stays in hospital. However, his literary output was significant and included several poetry collections, five novels, eight collections of short stories and two poem-plays, as well as non-fiction portraits of Orkney, an autobiography, *For the Islands I Sing* (1997), and published journalism. His final novel, *Beside the Ocean of Time* (1994) was shortlisted for the Booker Prize and was awarded the prize for Scottish Book of the Year by the Saltire Society.

George Bruce (1909–2002) was born in Fraserburgh and studied literature at the University of Aberdeen, graduating in 1932. He worked as a teacher in Dundee until 1947 when he took a post as a BBC producer working in Aberdeen and then Edinburgh. His earliest collection of poems *Sea Talk* (1944) was followed by six further collections of poetry and several volumes of prose. He was awarded an honorary D.Litt from the University of Aberdeen in 2000.

Agnes C. Carnegie was born and brought up in Aberdeen. However, she travelled widely throughout Europe and in Japan, where she taught English at the University of the Sacred Heart in Tokyo. Later in life, she converted to the Roman Catholic Church. Her poems were published in two volumes, *The Hours are Measured* (1948) and *The Timeless Flow* (1985).

Stewart Conn was born in Glasgow in 1936 and has for many years lived in Edinburgh. From 2002 to 2005 he was the capital's first official makar. Poetry publications include *Stolen Light: Selected Poems* and *Ghosts at Cockrow* and *The Loving Cup*: and as editor, *100 Favourite Scottish Poems* and *100 Favourite Scottish Love Poems*.

Robert Crawford was born in 1959. He is Professor of Modern Scottish Literature at St Andrews University. His books include *Selected Poems* (2005) and *Full Volume* (2008). His prose books include *Scotland's Books* (2007) and his biography of Robert Burns, *The Bard* (2009). His father grew up in Alford, recited the poetry of Charles Murray, and worked in Aberdeen in the 1930s.

Helen B. Cruickshank (1886–1975) was born and brought up near Montrose. After leaving school, she entered the civil service working first in London then in Edinburgh. She was a suffragette, a Scottish nationalist, and a member of the Saltire Society. She encouraged the work of other Scottish writers, such as Lewis Grassic Gibbon and Marion Angus, as well as publishing several volumes of her own work in both English and Scots.

Peter Davidson is Professor of Renaissance Studies and Honorary Keeper of the Renaissance collections at the University of Aberdeen. His publications include

The Palace of Oblivion (2007), *The Idea of North* (2005) and *The Lost City: Old Aberdeen* (2008). He is also a regular contributor to *PN Review.*

William Dunbar (c. 1460-1520) was probably born in East Lothian and is thought to have been a member of the noble house of Dunbar. He studied at the University of St Andrews where he took a master's degree in 1479. He then travelled in Europe before serving as a priest and diplomat in the court of James IV. In 1501, Dunbar accompanied the Archbishop of Glasgow on a visit to London to arrange the King's marriage to Margaret Tudor. During this visit he was dubbed the Rhymer of Scotland. Dunbar visited Aberdeen with Queen Margaret in 1511.

Joyce Everill (1921–2001) was born Joyce Mitchell in Cellardyke, Fife, and moved to Aberdeen where her father worked as a trawlerman. In 1941 while serving in the Anti-Aircraft Battery, she met her husband, Bob Everill. They had two daughters and a son. She started writing poetry in after her mother's death in 1983, and performed her work frequently around the city. She was the secretary of Aberdeen Writers' Circle, and in 1988 she won the Aberdeen Woman of the Year Award.

G. S. Fraser (1915–80) was born in Glasgow, grew up in Aberdeen and studied at the University of St Andrews. After serving in the British Army in North Africa in World War II, he returned to London where he became a journalist and critic. He was the Cultural Advisor to the UK Liason mission in Tokyo between 1949 and 1951. In 1959 he took an academic post at the University of Leicester where he taught until 1979.

Olive Fraser (1909–77) was born in Torry and brought up in Nairn by her great aunt. She studied at Aberdeen University then Girton College Cambridge where she won the Chancellor's Medal for English verse. Her adult life was plagued by poor health, due to a thyroid condition that was incorrectly diagnosed for thirty years. However, she continued to write and publish. In the 1960s she moved back to Aberdeen and enjoyed a spell of untroubled health in her later years. Her collected poems were edited by Helen Shire and published as *The Wrong Music* (1989).

Flora Garry (1900–2000) was born Flora MacDonald Campbell in New Deer, Aberdeenshire. Her parents owned a farm but her father was also a journalist and her mother wrote radio plays. She studied at Peterhead Academy and the University of Aberdeen. She then trained and worked as a teacher before marrying the distinguished physiologist Robert Campbell Garry. She wrote vividly about the Buchan landscape and culture in several volumes of poetry. She was awarded an honorary degree by the University of Aberdeen in 1999.

Arthur Geddes (1895–1968) was the son of Patrick Geddes, the influential urban sociologist. Arthur Geddes made a career as a distinguished geographer, working first in India and France and later in Scotland at the University of Edinburgh. He published translations of Gaelic songs from the Highlands and Islands in *The Songs of Craig and Ben* (1961). He also translated some of the Bengali songs of Rabindranath Tagore.

Eddie Gibbons was born in Liverpool and now lives in Aberdeen. He has published widely in newspapers, magazines and anthologies. He has published three collections of poetry including *Stations of the Heart* and *The Republic of Ted*. His latest book is *What They Say About You* (2009). He was prizewinner in the inaugural Edwin Morgan International Poetry Competition, 2008.

Donald Gordon (1921–85) was born in Aberdeen. Educated at Robert Gordon's College and the University of Aberdeen, he joined the Diplomatic Service after wartime service in the Royal Artillery, retiring in 1981 as HM Ambassador to Austria. *The Gangrel Fiddler and Other Poems* was published in 1984 and *The Low Road Home* posthumously in 1987.

George Gordon, Lord Byron (1788–1824) was born in London but his mother moved back to her home city of Aberdeen in 1789 to escape debts amassed by Byron's father. Until the age of ten, Byron lived in Queen Street and Broad Street and was educated at Aberdeen Grammar School. On the death of his great-uncle in 1798, he inherited the title of Sixth Baron Byron of Rochdale. After this he moved with his mother to Newstead Abbey and was educated at Harrow and Cambridge. After university he embarked on a life of aristocratic decadence and literary brilliance that made him one of the most celebrated figures of his generation. Byron's epic poem *Don Juan* was left uncompleted when Byron died of a fever while engaged in the fight for Greek independence.

George Gunn was born in Thurso in 1956. For seven years until the mid-1980s he worked on drilling rigs in the North and Irish seas. He is a well-known poet and playwright having written over twenty stage plays and several dramas for the BBC. He is currently artistic director of Grey Coast Theatre Company which is based in Caithness. His latest collection of poems is *The Atlantic Forest* (2008).

Thomas Hardy (1840–1928) was born in Higher Bockhampton near Dorchester and, apart from a few years in London as a young man, spent most of his life in Dorset. He trained as an architect but quickly made a name for himself as a novelist. He did not publish any poems until he was in his late fifties, when he gave up writing fiction and dedicated the last thirty years of his life to poetry. In all, he wrote fourteen novels and almost a thousand poems. Hardy visited Aberdeen in 1905 to receive an honorary degree from the University of Aberdeen.

George Rowntree Harvey lived in Aberdeen. His first book of poems Green Ears (1914) was followed by a book of war poems *Comrades! My Comrades!* (1919) and a range of plays and travel books, including *The Book of Scotland* (1949).

Seamus Heaney was born in Mossbawn, Northern Ireland in 1939. He was educated at Queen's University, Belfast, where he later lectured in English. He also taught at the University of California, Harvard University and the University of Oxford where he was professor of poetry from 1989 to 1994. He has written numerous volumes of poetry and literary criticism, and was awarded the Nobel Prize for Literature in 1995. He now lives in Dublin.

Dorothy E. Henderson (1910–86) was born Dorothy McLean. She attended the University of Aberdeen between 1926 and 1930.

Hazel Hutchison was born in Glasgow in 1968 and studied at the University of Edinburgh. She moved to Aberdeen in 1990 and worked as a journalist on the *Press and Journal* before studying for a PhD at the University of Aberdeen where she now lectures in the English Department. She has published poems, articles and books in Britain and the US.

Mick Imlah (1956–2009) was born and brought up near Glasgow and later in Kent. He was educated at Magdalen College, Oxford, where he subsequently taught as a Junior Fellow. He was editor of *Poetry Review* from 1983 to 1986, and then Poetry Editor at the *Times Literary Supplement* for sixteen years from 1992. He published several collections of poetry and co-edited *The New Penguin Book of Scottish Verse* (2006) with Robert Crawford. His final collection, *The Lost Leader*, was shortlisted for the T. S. Eliot Prize, and won the Forward Prize for Best Collection in 2008.

May C. Jenkins was educated at Aberdeen Girls' High School and Aberdeen University, after which she became a teacher of speech and drama at the Convent School Queen's Cross. She then became a journalist with Aberdeen Journals and for some years she bred cats. She has published poems, articles and short stories both in Britain and abroad. She reads and travels.

Jackie Kay was born in 1961 and brought up in Glasgow. Her first collection of poetry, *The Adoption Papers*, (1991) won a Forward Prize, a Saltire Award and a Scottish Arts Council Book Award. Her novel *Trumpet* won the Guardian

Fiction Award. Her collection of short stories *Wish I Was Here* won the Decibel Prize of the Year. She teaches at the University of Newcastle and lives in Manchester.

Jessie Kesson (1916–94) was born Jessie Grant Macdonald in Inverness and grew up in poverty in Elgin. At the age of ten, she was taken into care at an orphanage at Skene, near Aberdeen. Refused permission by the orphanage to take the entrance exams to the University of Aberdeen, Kesson turned herself into a successful author and broadcaster, producing poetry, plays and four volumes of fiction, as well as maintaining a career as a writer and producer for both radio and television. She was awarded an honorary degree by the University of Aberdeen in 1987.

Christine Laennec was born in 1960 in Portland, Oregon, and has made her home in Scotland. She has published short stories and poems in Scottish anthologies and literary publications including *Spring Tides, Northwards* and *Pushing Out the Boat*. Her work explores questions of place, adoption and identity. Novel-writing is currently her main focus.

William Ferguson McCorkindale was the author of several collections of verse published in Aberdeen, including *Fragments Against Ruin* (1969) and *The Mirror and the Maze* (1979).

Hugh McDiarmid (1892–1978) was born Christopher Murray Grieve in Langholme in the Scottish Borders. He worked as a journalist both before and after serving in the Royal Medical Corps during World War I. In the early 1920s MacDiarmid was living in Montrose, where he fostered a friendship with Lewis Grassic Gibbon. His major poetic work *A Drunk Man Looks at the Thistle* was published in 1926. He moved frequently, living in St Andrews, Glasgow, Whalsay, Ebbw Vale and London, but later in life he returned to the Scottish Borders. His cottage in Biggar is now run as a writers' centre. MacDiarmid was also active in left-wing politics and was a founder member of the Scottish Nationalist Party.

Donald MacEwan wrote the poem 'Aberdeen Chicago Arbroath' for a poetry competition in Aberdeen in the 1980s. It was first published in *A Hairst o' Words*, edited By Hellen Matthews (1991).

Ronald Campbell MacFie (1867–1931) grew up in Aberdeen, and trained as a physician. He had a dual career as a poet and popular scientific writer, publishing widely on both subjects. His volumes of poetry included *Granite Dust* (1892). He also wrote an appreciation of the life and work of William Watson. MacFie later lived in London, where he became the literary mentor to Flora Thomson, author of *Lark Rise to Candleford*.

G. A. McIntyre was born in 1925 and lived in Aberdeen.

Alastair Mackie (1925–95) was born in Aberdeen. He attended Skene Street School and later was awarded a scholarship to Robert Gordon's College. After naval war service, he graduated from the University of Aberdeen. He then taught English at Stromness Academy from 1951 to 1959, latterly settling in Anstruther, Fife, where he taught at Waid Academy until he retired in 1984.

Kevin MacNeil was born on the Isle of Lewis. He has published several volumes of verse in English and Gaelic, including *Love and Zen in the Outer Hebrides* (2001). His first novel *The Stornoway Way* was published in 2006.

Gerald Mangan is a Scottish poet, journalist, painter and part-time musician, resident in Paris. Poetry collections include *Waiting for the Storm* (1990). He has also written stage-plays including *Crying Wolf* (Communicado), and illustrated books include *The Sonnet History of Modern Poetry*. The latest exhibition of his literary portraits was held at the South Bank Centre in London.

Cate Marvin is the author of two poetry collections, *World's Tallest Disaster* (2001) and *Fragment of the Head of a Queen* (2007), and co-editor with Michael Dumanis of the anthology *Legitimate Dangers* (2006). She is the recipient of the Kathryn A. Morton Prize, the Kate Tufts Discovery Prize, and a Whiting Award. She is presently an associate professor in creative writing at the College of Staten Island, City University of New York.

Edwin Morgan was born in Glasgow in 1920. He was educated at the University of Glasgow, interrupting his studies to serve in the Royal Army Medical Corps during WWII. He returned to the University as a lecturer in 1947. He was visiting professor at Strathclyde University from 1987 to 1990. He has published numerous volumes of verse, prose and drama, and translations of *Beowulf* and Latin-American verse.

Ken Morrice (1924–2002) was born in Aberdeen. From his schooldays at Robert Gordon's College, he wrote verse all his life. A medical graduate of the University of Aberdeen, he later specialised in psychiatry. Seven volumes of his poetry were published and his verses appeared in many magazines and anthologies. He was married with three children.

Peter Mowat lived in Aberdeen in the 1960s and 1970s. His work was published in *Setting Out: New Poems from Aberdeen* (1972).

Robin Munro was born on the Island of Bute in 1946. His schooldays were spent in Wigtonshire, the Borders and Aberdeen, and he graduated from the University of Aberdeen. His poetry collections include *Shetland Like the World* and *The Land of the Mind*. He now runs a bookshop in Gatehouse of Fleet.

Geoffrey A. Oelsner lives in Arkansas in the USA. He was an American exchange student at the University of Aberdeen during the academic year 1969–70 and wrote 'Song for Aberdeen' shortly before the end of his stay. It was awarded the Calder verse prize in 1970. A psychotherapist by profession, he is also a singer-songwriter as well as a poet. His latest book of poetry is *Native Joy: poems songs visions dreams* (2004).

Wayne Price was born in south Wales in 1965 and now lives in Aberdeen. He has published prize-winning short stories and poetry in a number of anthologies and literary journals in the UK, Ireland and America. In 2008 he was runner-up in the inaugural Edwin Morgan International Poetry Competition. He teaches literature and creative writing at the University of Aberdeen.

Thomas Rist was born in 1971. He lectures in English at the University of Aberdeen. Publishing poems occasionally, he is also author of two books of criticism: *Shakespeare's Romances and the Politics of the Counter-Reformation* (1999) and *Revenge Tragedy and the Drama of Commemoration in Reforming England* (2008). He was winner of the Scottish Mountaineer's Poetry Competition 2005.

Gerard Rochford lives in Scotland 'where the best footballers leave and the best poets stay'. He has published widely in Scotland and Canada. His collections of poetry include *Eating Eggs with Strangers*, *The Holy Family and Other Poems* and *Figures of Stone*. His work was listed in Janice Galloway's *Best 20 Scottish Poems of 2006* for the Scottish Poetry Library.

Robin Robertson was born in 1955 and brought up in Aberdeen. His last collection, *Swithering*, was chosen as the Scottish Poetry Book of the Year and won the 2006 Forward Prize for Best Collection.

Alexander Scott (1920–89) was born and educated in Aberdeen. When WWII broke out in 1939 he interrupted his degree and enlisted with the Gordon Highlanders. He was later awarded the M.C. for distinguished service. After graduating in 1947, he took up a post at the University of Edinburgh, and from there moved to Glasgow, where he was instrumental in establishing the Department of Scottish Literature. He served as its head until his retirement. He published seven volumes of verse during his lifetime and left another *Incantations* unfinished at his death. He also wrote a biography of William Soutar, *Still Life* (1958).

John Sinclair was a student at Aberdeen University in the early 1970s. His work was published in *Setting Out: New Poems from Aberdeen* (1972).

J. Scott Skinner (1843–1927) was born and brought up in Banchory, and was taught to play the violin and cello by his older brother, after the death of their father. He was educated in Aberdeen and then trained as a professional musician in Manchester. He also trained as a dancing master and moved back to Aberdeenshire, where he taught dancing to the Royal household at Balmoral, and performed as a fiddler in the North-East of Scotland. He was celebrated as an arranger of folk tunes and as a composer of original songs and tunes, of which 'The Bonny Lass of Bon Accord' is the most famous.

Einarr Skúlason (born c. 1090) was an Icelandic priest and *skald*, or court poet. For most of his life he lived in at the court in Norway, working for the kings Sigurðr Jórsalafari and Haraldr Gilli. He later became marshall for Haraldr Gilli's son Eysteinn, whose raid on Aberdeen is recounted in the *Morkinskinna*.

Harry Smart was born in the North of England, and studied at the University of Aberdeen. He has published two volumes of poetry, *Pierrot* (1991) and *Fool's Pardon* (1995), and a novel *Zaire* (1998). He lives in Montrose.

Iain Crichton Smith (1928–98) was born in Glasgow and was brought up by his widowed mother in Bayble, Lewis. He studied at the University of Aberdeen and after doing National Service worked as an English teacher in Clydebank, Dumbarton and Oban. In 1977 he retired from teaching to write full-time, creating both poetry and fiction. Smith's writing won him several literary prizes and Saltire Society and Scottish Arts Council awards and fellowships. He was also awarded honorary doctorates from the Universities of Glasgow, Dundee and Aberdeen.

Alan Spence was born in Glasgow and is a novelist, poet, short-story writer and dramatist. He was named Scottish Writer of the Year in 1996 and won the Glenfiddich Spirit of Scotland Award in 2006. He is known for his novels, such as *The Pure Land, The Magic Flute* and *Way to Go,* and his collections of haiku, *Glasgow Zen* and *Clear Light*. He is also Professor of Creative Writing at the University of Aberdeen, where he is the director of the Word Festival.

Anne Stevenson was born in England to American parents, grew up in New England and in Ann Arbor, Michigan, and has spent most of her adult life in England. She has published fourteen volumes of verse including *Stone Milk* (2007). She has also written about the life and work of Elizabeth Bishop and Sylvia Plath. In 2007 she was awarded a Lifetime Achievement Award from the Lannan Foundation.

Rachel Annand Taylor (1876–1960) was a distinguished scholar and poet, who published several volumes of verse and studies of the Italian Renaissance and the poet William Dunbar. She was one of the earliest female students to attend the University of Aberdeen between 1894 and 1897, but she did not graduate. After marrying Alexander Taylor, she moved to Dundee and then to London. In 1943 she was awarded an honorary degree by the University of Aberdeen to mark the fiftieth anniversary of the admission of women students.

Tim Tricker grew up in Suffolk. His poetry has been variously published in magazines and anthologies. He also writes plays, many of which have been performed by companies in Scotland. He has a PhD in the poetry of Ted Hughes, and currently teaches literature at the University of Aberdeen.

Sue Vickerman is from Angus. She wrote two collections of poetry Shag (2003) and The Social Decline of the Oystercatcher (2005) from an Aberdeenshire lighthouse. She has also published poems in a wide range of journals, and has received English and Scottish Arts Council grants. She currently lives in Yorkshire and is working on a novel Special Needs.

Roderick Watson was born in Aberdeen in 1943 and educated at Aberdeen Grammar School, the University of Aberdeen and the University of Cambridge. At Stirling University he has lectured and published widely on modern Scottish literature, and currently co-edits the Journal of Stevenson Studies. His main poetry collections are True History on the Walls (1977) and Into the Blue Wavelengths (2004).

William Watson (1858–1935) was born in Yorkshire. His first volume of poetry The Prince's Quest appeared in 1880. He was recommended for Poet Laureate but was granted a Civil List pension instead. The University of Aberdeen awarded him an honorary LL.D. in 1904. In later life, he lived in Sussex.

Acknowledgements

The editors would like to thank the many people who have supported and assisted this project. These include: the editorial team at Polygon; Lizzie MacGregor, Julie Johnston and the staff of the Scottish Poetry Library, Edinburgh; the staff of the City Library, Aberdeen; the staff of Historic Collections at the University of Aberdeen; colleagues in the Department of English, especially Derrick Mc-Clure, Isobel Murray and Tarrin Wills; Karen Scaife and the administrative staff of the Word Festival; Hellen Matthews, Ian Olson and Gerard Rochford for help tracing copyrights; and Vice-Principal, Professor Chris Gane for his support of the project from its early stages.

We also acknowledge permission to reproduce the following poems: Marion Angus, 'George Gordon, Lord Byron, Aberdeen, 1924' from *The Tinker's Road* (1924) and 'The Silver City' from *Sun and Candlelight* (1927) by permission of Alan J. Byatt; Meg Bateman, 'Buntàt' is Sgadan / Tatties and Herring' from *Soirbeas / FairWind* (2007) by permission of Meg Bateman; Sheena Blackhall, 'Brig O' Balgownie', 'North East Toun', 'Gates of St Machar Cathedral', and 'The Well at King's' from *Skin Balaclavas* (2000) by permission of Sheena Blackhall; George Mackay Brown, 'Foresterhill (1992)', from *Collected Poems* (2005) by permission of the Estate of George Mackay Brown; George Bruce, 'Aberdeen, The Granite City', 'Envoi' and 'Old Snapshot' from *Today Tomorrow: The Collected Poems of George Bruce,* by permission of the Estate of George Bruce; Stewart Conn, 'Roull of Corstorphine' from *Ghosts at Cockcrow* (2005) by permission of Bloodaxe Books; Robert Crawford, 'Aberdeen' from *The Tip of My Tongue* (2003) and 'Aberdeenshire' from *Selected Poems* (2005) both by permission of Random House Group Ltd; Peter Davidson, 'Aberdeenshire Elegy' by permission of Peter Davidson; Joyce Everill 'Birthin Place' from *Granny's Button Box* (1989) by permission of Corine Graham; G. S. Fraser, 'Home Town Elegy' and 'Lean Street' from *The Poems of G. S. Fraser* (1981) by permission of Eileen Fraser; Flora Garry, 'The Professor's Wife' and 'Rostov-on-Don (1942)' from *Collected Poems* (1995) by permission of Steve Savage Publishers; Arthur Geddes, 'Brig o' Balgownie' by permission of Colin Geddes; Eddie Gibbons, 'At Melting Point' and 'The Marginal Fields' from *Stations of the Heart* by permission of Eddie Gibbons; Donald Gordon, 'Lang Journey Back', 'Cultural Revolution' and 'Battle Sang O the Reid Army' from *The Low Road Home* (1987) by permission of Molly Gordon; George Gunn, 'Piper: For the 167 dead of the Piper "Alpha"' from *Sting* (1991) by permission of George Gunn; Seamus Heaney, 'Granite Chip' from *Opened Ground* (1998) by permission of Faber and Faber Ltd; Mick Imlah, 'John Imlah' from *The Lost Leader* (2008) by permission of Faber and Faber Ltd; May C. Jenkins, 'Roads in Rain' by permission of May C. Mackay; Jackie Kay, 'Old Aberdeen' from 'Life Mask' (2005) by permission of Jackie Kay; Jessie